AF573689

The Man in the Middle

To my mother,
Laura Doreen Bevan

Derek Bevan

The Man in the Middle

seren

seren is the book imprint of
Poetry Wales Press Ltd
Nolton Street, Bridgend, CF31 3BN Wales
www.seren-books.com

Second impression, 2001

ISBN 1-85411-290-2

A CIP record for this title is available from the British Library

Cover: Kevin Moseley gets his marching orders, Newbridge vs Pontypool, 30 December 1983 (courtesy of the *Western Mail*)

The publisher works with the financial assistance of the Arts Council of Wales

Printed in Wales by CPD, Ebbw Vale

Contents

Beginnings

In 1972 refereeing was the last thing on my mind. I was twenty-five years old, working in Brynlliw Colliery near Grovesend and enjoying life playing flanker for my village club, the Vardre. Although my rugby playing career wasn't going any further it was everything I wanted it to be. And I was quite happy to be working underground; both my brothers worked underground so it was a case of following in a family tradition. Although they were the worst working conditions, they were the best-paid apprenticeships. My father certainly wasn't happy for me to work underground because he'd spent all his working life there. He had begged me not to go there but like all teenage sons I thought I knew better. The camaraderie in the colliery was an incredible experience. I worked with people from Penclawdd, Pontarddulais, Gowerton and Morriston and there was damn good banter on a Monday, especially if we'd been playing against each other the previous Saturday. Rugby was THE sport underground.

I was an electrician and my job was to maintain power to the plough system which cut the coal from the face onto a conveyor and onto the belts. The plough and conveyors were all electrically driven so there was a lot of switchgear in the roadways along with signaling and emergency systems. If there was a breakdown the electricians had to get things going as soon as possible. Time was money and if these machines weren't working the management would take it into consideration when monthly efficiency targets were reviewed.

On a particular day in October we had been having trouble with the roof and I happened to be repairing one of the signaling stations underneath the problem area. There wasn't a warning. Normally in the older faces, you would hear the timber prop shafts creaking, but we had hydraulic metal supports so there wasn't any time to move if they gave way. It was a Tuesday afternoon shift and I was on a face too low to stand up in. So I was on my hands and knees repairing a signal unit about eight inches from the floor. It happened so quickly. I heard a rumble and three large pieces came loose, hit the spill pan which stopped the coal falling off the conveyor belt, and came down on to my back. I was only stuck there for about two minutes but it seemed like an eternity. I couldn't panic because I couldn't move. Luckily there were a couple of workers nearby. They'd heard the fall, knew something had happened to me and were there quickly.

I was very pale, almost white because I'd had a tremendous fright. They got me out into the roadway and although I could stand my back was bad. I couldn't feel any pain, only numbness. The pain came the following day when all the bruising came out. Getting ready to go to the surface, I didn't realize that this would be a life-changing event. I was more concerned about whether I would be fit enough for the Vardre for the Saturday. I walked out of the pit and had a shower before going home.

As I'd been involved in an accident underground I had to have a medical check-up and the specialist I saw said that it would take two years for me to recover. I was advised not to play any sort of contact sport for that period. It wasn't a specific injury but it has affected the way I run ever since. I wasn't too upset at the time. At first I thought the accident was far more serious so to be told that I would be making a full recovery was good news in itself. I thought then that I would join the Vardre committee. All clubs look for committeemen so perhaps I could make my contribution to the club by sweeping the dressing rooms, selling raffle tickets, serving behind the bar – all the usual things that are required. But I didn't enjoy it at all. The players would come in to the clubhouse after a match full of talk and chat about the incidents in the game and because I wasn't a part of it I found myself getting ratty. I couldn't sell raffle tickets while the players were enjoying themselves! I needed some action. After just a couple of weeks I realized that the next two years were going to be long ones. I even thought about going back to the specialist and knocking my rehabilitation down to twelve months at most!

Evan Dan was chairman of the Vardre at the time and also District E Member of the WRU and served on the International Referees Panel. A former referee himself, it was he who suggested I should have a go at refereeing. I laughed at him! I'd never done a minute's refereeing. In fact I bloody hated referees, I had no time for them at all. I'd been sent off twice and becoming a referee hadn't even entered my head. I thoroughly enjoyed my rugby as a player. You were a part of a team and the thought of going on your own to a rugby club didn't sound like a very good idea at all. But Evan told me to contact Marsden Bidder, the Secretary of the Swansea and District League. Marsden is probably the greatest servant the District has ever had and, like most leagues at the time, it were short of referees. I was welcomed with open arms. I explained to Marsden that, after two years, I would go back to playing. Marsden said he would be delighted if I could give him two seasons. He also told me that I might surprise myself and actually enjoy being in the middle, and that I might want to stick at it.

I received no training or instruction, I just jumped in at the deep end. Now there are well-structured course for budding referees, but I hadn't even run the line. My first game was Cwmgors Seconds against Trebanos Seconds – a local derby! I arrived at the clubhouse an hour and a half before kick off and the place was empty. A quick tour of Cwmgors showed me all the cafés were closed, so I sat in the car for forty minutes until people started to arrive. Among them was the late Winston Jones, one of the top refs in Wales at the time. He had a back injury and wasn't refereeing so he had come along to watch the game instead. I believe he was the financial adviser for Cwmgors.

The game was a trial, but I got through it. Naturally, I was called all the names under the sun. As we came off the field one of the Trebanos players shouted across to me and like a fool I turned around. "Bevan," he said, "you weren't much of a player – you're an even worse referee!" But Winston Jones had some words of comfort for me. He'd seen some promise but told me to concentrate on the basics and not to be too clever. For my part there was an obvious lack of knowledge of the laws. Instead I tried to understand what the players were attempting to do.

As far as the front row was concerned, I didn't have a clue. I'd only played there once when one of our side didn't turn up and, as the biggest in the back row, I had to move up. It wasn't a pleasant experience at all. I had a hiding and was pushed about like one of those bendy toys. It was a game against New Dock Stars and it took my opposite number about ten seconds to realize that he wasn't up against a regular prop forward, so I had a pasting. As a result when scrums were collapsing in my very first game as a referee, I didn't really know what was happening. Both sides were screaming for penalties. They knew I was a rookie. Second teams are usually made up of youngsters and some 'veterans' who tried to con me every step of the way, and probably succeeded. They still tease me in Trebanos to this day.

So I signed up for a referees course with Gwyn Watts, the sports master at Bishop Gore Grammar School in Swansea, and organiser of refereeing courses for beginners. There were six sessions, two nights a week at Bishop Gore School, at which I was amazed by what I learned about the laws of the game. There were some I didn't know existed, a revelation to me as a former captain of my village club! The course also involved a written exam. The pass mark was 90 per cent and I surprised myself with 98 per cent. After gaining more confidence in my knowledge of the laws, I actually began to enjoy refereeing. The course gave me more authority and now I was looking forward to a Saturday, and to receiving my fixture list.

Odd misunderstandings still occurred as I took up the challenge. I remember arriving in Brynamman for a game and a committee-man directing me to the visitors' changing room because it was quite unusual to have a twenty-six year old taking charge of the game. I told him I was the referee. "What's the matter with you then, why aren't you playing?" came the curt reply. Club officials got to know me and I found that I was being given some of the better District matches as I improved. I'd learned all the laws by now, and in rugby they are laws, not rules. Laws are there to be obeyed whereas rules are made to be broken which is exactly what I used to do as a player!

Rugby was my game. I was born in Clydach and have lived there all my life. I was the youngest of four children, three boys and a girl. My father was a big Swansea football supporter but he did turn up to watch a rugby game one day when I was captain of the Vardre and my brother Ken was captain of Glais. But being a soccer man he was bored to tears. (Glais beat us 14-3, and I gave away the first penalty for a late tackle on the outside half. We'd been told that there wasn't much 'bottle' in him so I thought I'd try him out early on but it cost us three points.)

School for me was Clydach Infants, then the Juniors. I passed my eleven-plus and there was a choice of Ystalyfera Grammar School or Pontardawe. I chose Pontardawe, but just across the road was Pontardawe Tech where Gareth Edwards was studying. My first real taste of rugby came at the age of fourteen, playing in the Dewar Shield competition for Swansea Valley schools. Gareth played with us for a year. Even then you could see that Gareth was a special player, and the team revolved around him.

I'd got into the side as a winger but a year later Bill Samuel, the sports master at Pontardawe Technical College and committee member for Swansea Valley Schools told me I should move to flanker. I'd gone into the centre for a few games previously so it was apparent that I was slowing up! We'd beaten Swansea for the first time ever, but with plenty of help from a local referee. I'd produced some good tackling that match and was put in the back row because of it. Bill Sam told me that I was 'defensive' and not 'creative' so he said I would be used to 'destroy' rather than 'create'. That's where I remained throughout my playing career.

I graduated to the Vardre Youth and left school to begin my apprenticeship with the National Coal Board as an electrician. I had no academic qualifications and finished with school at fifteen. But I played alongside some real characters for the Vardre then, particularly for the first team. And I represented West Wales, which was a big deal in those days.

The West Wales League was a tremendous thing. Vardre, though, weren't that good and very often we were the chopping blocks for teams like Crynant, Pontarddulais and Hendy. These were all tough, hard games. I didn't have the dedication to make the step up to first class. I wasn't a man who would put in the effort to train. Even then you got out what you put in and I just didn't do it. I lacked the ambition to go any further and I was very happy just to play rugby with my mates from the village. I didn't want to play for anyone else. I was what you would describe as a 'robust player' and played as a blind-side flanker. Occasionally I would play on the open side but when I came up against the better players I went back to the blind because I wasn't quick enough to get near them.

And the future referee was sent off three times during my playing career, though only twice 'officially'. The first time was in Waunarlwydd: I was given my marching orders along with their prop for illegal use of the boot – allegedly. But both committees got together after the game and fed the referee with enough beer to convince him not to report the matter! He agreed that if it wasn't in the paper the following day, he wouldn't report it. There wasn't a local scribe about but if there had been I'm sure a large whisky would have kept him quiet! So I got away with that one. But on the next occasion I got an early shower, it was for the same offence, illegal use of the boot. The official was Brian Kelleher, who was an international referee, and who completely misread the incident in my opinion. Their player was head butting my toe! Kelleher called me back as I was walking off and I thought I'd got away with it again. But he just wanted to check he had the right name. That was against Trebanos and I got an extra fortnight's suspension because I was captain. But when we played Trebanos, anything went. It was all part and parcel of the game then – without any malice, of course.

I was sent off for the second time (or third, depending on how you view it) during a match against Seven Sisters. Again, the game was deteriorating and the referee had to make an example of someone – and that someone happened to be me. What we actually did was nothing really. Their open-side flanker and I were fighting toe to toe. No-one else was involved and it was more like *Come Dancing* really, but the ref had already given a warning. What had gone on before had been far worse but the time had come for him to take positive and decisive action.

When I started refereeing, I realised that I had to improve my fitness as well as my knowledge of the laws. But being a ref I had to go out on my own and it wasn't until then that I became ambitious and dedicated in the world of rugby. I began running three or four nights a week. I spoke with other referees to pick up tips and worked hard at being better. Strangely, I was fitter as a referee than I ever was as a player. But I still missed the team element of rugby and I started a habit early on that I always kept up of returning to the Vardre on a Saturday night after a game. Vardre became more and more successful after the split up of the West Wales League and I had to miss out on some great days at the club because I'd be refereeing elsewhere! We played Pontypool and Bridgend in the cup, and we hosted Newbridge when one of their players received lime burns from the pitch markings! Newport came to the village and we would have played Cardiff in 1997 but there was a mess up with a draw.

I sent off my first player during a Youth Cup game in Penclawdd. He was a home player called Richard Jones who was due to have a trial for Wales the following week. It was for illegal use of the boot, and I had no choice. He was automatically banned and wasn't able to take part in the trial. The Penclawdd club, to say the least, were not happy. In fact they were downright critical. That occasion was the first hard time I'd had from club officials. Perhaps I'd had it too easy until then. I'd been refereeing players I'd previously played against and things had gone well. I could enjoy a pint in the clubhouse after the game with them and there'd been no problems. But the reaction to the sending off made me realize I'd crossed a line. The home club treasurer was responsible for the referee's expenses in those days. It was six shillings and he came into the dressing room and threw the money on the chair so the coins bounced all over the floor. "I hope we never see you again," he said, and walked out! When I walked into the bar people turned their backs on me. Nobody offered to buy me a pint.

The boy missed the trial. But when you went to your monthly District Referees' meeting you found out that all referees had these experiences. Players could do no wrong in the eyes of their clubs, and committees would always support their own players against any refereeing decision. I should have known this because my own club Vardre did the same. Penclawdd was the game at which I found out that making the popular decisions is easy but the unpopular ones are the hard ones to make. This had been during a Youth match where there'd been only thirty or forty spectators!

I had had that kind of learning experience with the Swansea and District for two and a half seasons when, in the 1974-75 season I received a letter informing me I was to be put on the probation grade. There were only five grades then, one to four and the probationary grade. This meant that I would do my normal games in the District and be given at least one game a month of WRU status which were first team matches. So that could be West Wales League or East Wales. I would have an assessor who would report back to the WRU and this assessment, of course, now had immense importance. The assessor could decide which way my career went. Not many people went on probation twice. The structure was that usually you had six games or so to make your mark. If you had one bad game and five good ones this would be taken into account. The assessor was completely neutral and there to watch you as a referee.

Thankfully my probationary games went well. I had already passed my own two year deadline and had given up any thoughts of going back to play. I was twenty-seven years old, really enjoying refereeing and by now I also had three small children aged five, three and three (the twins!). I was working for an electrical contractor so I couldn't afford to incur another injury – I returned to the Vardre club after one game to learn that one of my back row mates, Wynford, had been carted off to hospital with a double leg fracture. A nasty injury would badly affect my family.

As a referee I was going to clubs and starting to become successful at it: my reputation was growing. I was being welcomed around south Wales; mind you, all club secretaries are 'sioni pob ochor', they like to butter up the referee! When I would return to the Vardre the boys would ask me how my game had gone. Although I wasn't a player there anymore I was talking with the players again. During training they would ask me where I was refereeing on Saturday.

At least they were taking an interest in what I was doing. Personally, I still had no inkling of where it would lead me. I went to Seven Sisters the week after Meirion Joseph, the international referee, and the committeemen there reminded me about this, which made me question whether I was up to it. Nobody knew who I was! But these things gave you a lift. I could tell the boys in the Vardre with pride then that I was going to Seven Sisters, and that the highly respected Meirion Joseph had been there only the previous week!

My refereeing ambitions reflected my playing ones to a certain extent because all I wanted in the first years was to be a damn good West Wales referee. I'd been brought up in that League and I thought it was the best rugby in south Wales. It was fabulous rugby to play in, superbly organized with great committees and forty committed clubs involved. There were really hard men playing who took no prisoners. But then I started to think what the next refereeing step might be. There were always two tiers to the top flight in Welsh rugby. At the top were the likes of Cardiff, Swansea, Llanelli, Neath and Newport. But you also had Penarth, Tredegar, Abertillery below. I thought that maybe I could make it in the lower tier. Then, unexpectedly, in 1975 I was given Neath against Resolven in a centenary game and the opportunity to referee on the Gnoll, a ground at which I had played. It wasn't a big crowd, of course, but international players like Scotland's Wilson Lauder played for Neath. So back at the Vardre I could now start to name drop! It's an awful thing: I must have mentioned him about a thousand times and bored everyone. But I loved it.

In 1978-79 I went up to Grade Two and started to referee teams like Penarth, Abertillery and Glamorgan Wanderers on a regular basis. The clubs weren't greatly supported. Probably the same number would turn out to see Pontarddulais playing on a Saturday and I tried to referee in the same style as I had on the previous grade. The international referee Denzil Lloyd had advised me to do just this. His view was that if I was climbing the ladder it was because I was doing well as I was.

The jump from Grade Two to One was a different matter. Up there were the Llanellis and Cardiffs, big clubs with big crowds which create a different sort of pressure on a referee. There were a lot of complaints from the smaller clubs at the time that there were double standards among referees. They felt that the so-called 'first class clubs' were allowed to get away with things that the smaller clubs weren't.

I still hadn't refereed the big names on a regular basis until I made it to Grade One in the 1979-80 season. Now I was visiting clubs like Pontypool and refereeing their famous front row, along with Terry Cobner in the back row and John Perkins in the second row. In Bridgend J.P.R. Williams was the full back. Aberavon had a marvellous team. I was now rubbing shoulders with players I'd looked up to. In the beginning I was over-awed. I still recall the thrill when I first stood in the tunnel in Stradey Park waiting to take the field. I was refereeing Llanelli for the first time, against Glamorgan Wanderers. The fixture had come as a surprise to me because I was given the match at short notice when someone had cried off. It was a Tuesday night match and Phil Bennett and Ray Gravell were playing. To think I would be running on the same field as Phil Bennett was beyond my wildest dreams. J.J. Williams was also in the team. There was a moment in the tunnel before we went out onto the field when I became quite choked. I remembered telling my late father that I was taking up refereeing and how he'd laughed. I wished he could have been alive then to see me run out onto Stradey Park; soccer man or not he would have been so proud of me.

I was in a complete daze, I can't remember how I got through the game. I must have penalised the poor Glamorgan Wanderers open-side flanker a dozen times for tackling Phil Bennett. I thought that he could never be quick enough to tackle Phil so he must be offside! I waited in the clubhouse long enough afterwards to meet the players, but I was busting to get back to the Vardre to tell the boys I'd been refereeing Phil and Ray and how I had to tell them to get back onside or I'd have to penalise them! It was almost like a dream, and the boys saying "Bev reffed in Llanelli" in almost mystical tones. A lot of the boys had turned up to watch me in Stradey and they all had a bollocking from the coach because they'd missed training!

First Internationals

My career continued. I gained experience and refereed the big Welsh clubs on a regular basis. Then came the final step up the ladder. At the time of my first international, world rugby still had the strange system of International Rugby Board countries and non-IRB countries. Caps were only awarded for internationals when countries played against each other in their respective groups. Consequently my first three international matches didn't count as 'proper' test matches, though they felt important enough to me. In 1984 I did Italy against Romania in the beautiful resort of L'Aquila, above Rome. This was a totally different experience to refereeing club rugby in Wales. The town mayor came to meet me at the airport in a chauffeur-driven limousine! The fixture felt like an international because I didn't know anyone and suddenly I was a stranger again. L'Aquila is in a rugby playing area and every billboard, hotel and newsagent had posters about the game. I was given an armed escort on to the pitch; the teams ran out and I started to follow them but a policeman stopped me and I was taken right to the touchline by the Carabinieri. At the final whistle they were waiting to escort me back to the dressing room. But there was no controversial incident or point of contention during the game, which Italy won 12-6. Perhaps the town of L'Aquila was so proud to be staging an international it wanted to make a big thing of it. My other two 'minor' internationals were the tests on Ireland's tour of Japan in 1985, of which more later.

Appointments to international matches then were allocated on a country by country basis. The IRB would appoint a country for an international and the Rugby Union of that country would then appoint their own officials. Wales would have possibly three internationals in a season so the refereeing would be shared out. Since 1985 was my first appointment I was given the less demanding fixture: Winston Jones and Clive Norling had the Five Nations matches that season. I'd known I was in with a shout. We had a meeting in the Police Club in Bridgend and Denzil Lloyd announced the international panel. We then discussed any other business and points of law but it all went over my head; I was on cloud nine. I was also wary, however. Despite the fact that I had now stepped up to the top level, I knew I could end up without actually refereeing an international. It had happened to Evan Dan of the Vardre who was appointed to the international panel but didn't referee. So I was delighted that my opportunity came around very quickly.

My first recognized international was England against Romania in front of a crowd of 30,000 at Twickenham on 5 January 1985. The ground was less than half full, Romania wasn't a big attraction and had no travelling support. Clive and Winston were my touch judges so I had plenty of advice from both of them. Thank goodness there were no 'talking flags' in those days! Not that those two needed them anyway. They were never short of things to say. Clive, unbelievably, was quite subdued when he ran touch. He enjoyed being in the middle, so running touch wasn't his favourite thing to do. By now he was a world-famous referee and certainly different to those that had gone before. When you arrived at your hotel people would push past you to shake his hand and engage him in a chat about the game. "Are you doing the game tomorrow Clive?" they would ask. "No," he would reply, "we've got to bring on the youngsters!" The autograph hunters would make a bee-line for him. It was a useful lesson because the same thing would happen to me later on in my career.

My preparations were quite low key. The system is laid out for you, and the referees and their partners are hosted by a liaison officer from the home union. That Saturday morning was bitterly cold. We got to the ground early and kept busy so there wasn't much time for me to think about the match and I wasn't very nervous. It was like being led on a leash. Clive and Winston had done it all before and I was almost in the background. England won the game quite convincingly although the score of 22-15 was close, but there were few talking points. It wasn't the end-to-end sort of rugby that you might dream of for your debut, quite the opposite. But the assessor gave me a 'B' for the game which was pleasing and a solid start. That evening I was all dressed up to go to the post-match function and I followed a group of England players in the hotel. I ended up at the England team's private presentation for new caps! I was in the wrong place but I was invited to stay. Two of the players receiving new caps that day were Rob Andrew and Wade Dooley. Rob had a nice cap which fitted him well. But Wade is so big the cap looked like a pimple on his head! For myself I now had a badge for my jersey and a tie as an international referee.

My second 'full' international also involved England, this time against France in Paris in 1986. It was a big match and a totally different experience. It was a step-up again, from a nice and easy introduction to a full house at the Parc des Princes. Philippe Dintrans was the French captain and Nigel Melville captained England. The French took the game to the English from the off and their flanker, Eric Champ, was outstanding. His nickname was 'Mad Eyes'. It was a super game full of open rugby. France scored one of their tries from inside their own 22 and it was a pleasure to watch. The crowd obviously loved it. There was a bit of a controversy when Stuart Barnes went for an interception one-handed in an overlap situation. He said the ball had gone up in the air but I said it had gone forward and I awarded a penalty try, much to the delight of the French crowd. In fairness to England they played their part in the match and Dooley got a try. Barnes gave me some stick afterwards and I also got some from a bunch of England supporters at the airport. Most of it was in good humour but some wasn't. You have to be above that because as soon as you stop to talk, others join in and it can quickly become very difficult. The referee doesn't decide which way a game is going to be played. He is there to apply the laws. But if a referee applies the laws in a hard, tight manner he can ruin a game. It's an awful thing to say, but that's how complicated our game has become. A bad referee can make a good game bad, but a good referee can't make a bad game good. In trying to make a poor game better there is a danger of allowing things to go. Then discipline begins to get worse and major problems can arise. At least if one side wants to keep on killing the ball they can now be penalised for persistent infringement.

My first experience of a tour as opposed to a single international match came in 1985 with the Irish in Japan. It was a strange baptism. There was precious little advertising of the tour. Although there are sixteen million people living in Tokyo alone very few of them were interested in rugby, unlike the Italians at L'Aquila. I refereed two tests in Japan, one in Osaka and one in Tokyo. The Japanese crowds have there own way of reacting when it comes to supporting rugby. There would be a passage of robust forward driving play with rucks and mauls. I would blow the whistle and there would be complete silence while the crowd waited for my decision. If it was a Japanese ball there would then be polite applause. It was amazing compared to the involvement of Welsh crowds. But the Japanese loved instances in the game which a European supporter wouldn't.

There was a little bit of foul play in the first match and Shiggy Konno, the President of the Japanese Rugby Union had publicly berated his players for losing so heavily. If this was a motivational tactic it seemed to work because in the second game they came out all fired up. It was certainly a different experience and felt more like a normal international. The Irish boys knew they'd been in a game. Even so the air of unreality continued at the after-match dinner in Tokyo when the Japanese players were presented with new caps. An Irish player who was sitting next to me told me that he wasn't getting one despite playing in the game, because the Irish Rugby Union didn't recognise it as a full international.

Since I'd refereed matches between two countries, *I* considered myself now to be an international referee. However, I wasn't officially recognised as such by the IRB because the matches involved weren't accorded full test match status. This made me even more determined to get a true international match under my belt and my ambition was fulfilled the following year.

I'd linked up with the Irish team in Heathrow Airport and was on the same flight as them to Japan. I sat next to second row forward Willie Anderson and within five or six hours it felt as if I was a part of the touring party. Camaraderie is an attractive part of rugby and the players, supporters and officials know where the lines are drawn between socialising and playing. I refereed the first Ireland match in Japan, in Morioka, then ran touch in their second game. I stayed in the same hotel as them, though on a different floor. I was eating in the same restaurants and having a drink in the same bars and being invited to the same functions. So it wasn't like refereeing an international, it was more like refereeing your mates! That made it more difficult for me. During the matches they wouldn't call me 'ref' it was "What was that for Derek?" By the second match it had even become 'Bev'!

Refereeing the Modern Game

I've always been ready to listen to advice. I haven't always agreed with it or taken it, but on my way up as a referee I knew when to stay tight-lipped when dealing with people in authority. I've never been shy but I feel I'm reserved in some ways, and I've never felt it's a good thing to shout the odds. All the referees have a different style and there have often been stronger personalities around than mine. Clive Norling was very talkative and forthcoming on and off the pitch. Winston Jones could have talked for Wales, he never stopped; he could talk underwater.

One of the great rules of refereeing (of life as well) is to be careful not to have an inflated opinion of yourself. You soon get caught out. While I was on the probation grade I was given a difficult cup replay in Gorseinon and approached it with the wrong attitude, believing I was above the standard of the game. I'd played against one of the Gorseinon players and ended up sending him off due to bad refereeing. He wasn't a dirty player but he was so frustrated by my decisions and cocksure attitude that he lost his cool. At the end of a game both sets of players clap the referee off the field but at Gorseinon they all turned their backs on me. A supporter called out "The WRU can keep him if that's the way he referees!" That rang in my ears all the way home and I vowed that it wouldn't happen again. I'd learned a salutary lesson.

Half past four on a Saturday afternoon or straight after a game isn't the best time to make decisions. It's not the best time for coaches to give press conferences or speak to players or have a go at the referee. Nobody has had time to reflect on the game or to cool down if they are annoyed or frustrated. There have been improvements in this area over the years. Today there is a code of conduct. The attitude of the players on the field is a lot better. Every game is now recorded on video by one or both clubs. The facility to cite has made a big difference, as has the development of professionalism. If a player loses his cool now he's liable to be hit in the pocket. The introduction of independent touch judges was a definite step forward. As a referee you could go to a club and have six good matches but if you have a bad one the club will remember. I've had some committeemen who have refused to run the line for me. You were very much on your own in the past. I've also had instances of penalty kicks at which one flag has been raised and one kept down. And you were aware of which clubs had representatives on the referees committee who could make life difficult for you. The pressure was high in the past.

As I developed I watched matches simply to see how other referees coped with different situations in a game. My speciality, as a former flanker, was looking out for the back rows. I watched them like a hawk and would pull them up for things I had done as a player – I was a poacher turned gamekeeper. The front row was a different matter. I had a good rapport with the flankers but the front three remained a mystery. I would sit with them in the bar after a game and try to learn what goes on there. Players like Meredydd James of Bridgend could talk for hours on the subject though they were careful not to mention the game I'd just refereed in case they gave something away. Of course, it's possible to sin bin props for continuous infringement these days. In the past it was a choice between many penalties or dismissal. At one time there wasn't even an appeals process for the player dismissed so that was another way to upset a club's committee and bring pressure on yourself.

People say that criticism is like water off a duck's back to a referee, but that's rubbish. All criticism hurts. I don't know of any referee who can shrug off criticism, we all go out to do as well as we can. I made some silly mistakes and some horrendous ones, and the crowd have been justified in jeering. People have approached me after a game and complained about a decision and I've told them "You're absolutely right". That usually takes the wind out of their sails. Another rule for referees: you've got to come clean. If you've made a mistake don't make another by trying to justify the first. It's not been easy, but I've apologized to coaches and players.

My preparations for a match on a Saturday depended on where it was played. Beforehand I usually went to see my mother who still lives nearby to see if she needed anything. I always got my kit out early. The boots were prepared on the previous Saturday night. I did my own laundry, and that was done the night after a game or the Sunday morning, ready for use on Monday if necessary. I could almost put on a clean jersey for every day of the month now. There are so many different competitions with many different sponsors I have to be careful to choose the correct one. You have to ensure that there are no colour clashes with either of the teams. I had to change my jersey during a game only once. It happened during the 1999-2000 season when Bridgend were playing at home to Glasgow. Bridgend came out in blue and Glasgow were in red. The pitch was very muddy and at half time, Bridgend changed to its yellow kit. This then clashed with me so I had to change to a green one. Spare kit is essential and there's plenty in the wardrobe nowadays. Normally the WRU supplies three different colours. Then there's the international kit, the IRB, the Cup. We've had Umbro, Cotton Traders, Reebok and Mizuno. We've been sponsored by Heineken and Admiral.

I liked to arrive at a game a minimum of an hour before kick off. If I hadn't been to that ground before I would set off earlier. Very often if I was too early I'd stop for a cup of coffee. I didn't like to be late. Dress code was collar and tie. If the pitch was near the clubhouse I checked to make sure that it was marked correctly and to see if it took a stud. The two touch judges (or three in premier matches) would arrive. Then the club coaches came to you to check things and perhaps try to influence you. Coaches have referees that they like and others that they don't. There are always little things that they want to let you know about the other side, what they believe went against them or what the opponents got away with in their last match and so on. Up until the 1999 World Cup, especially in Australia and New Zealand, coaches came to the hotel to have a meet with you and sometimes brought the assistant coach and the captain as well!

I see nothing wrong with it. I didn't get anything out of it myself. Though I looked forward to the first time it happened I found it became to be an inconvenience. It was too often an attempt to influence you in one direction or another. The only pre-match meeting I can look back on positively was with Pierre Berbizier in New Zealand in 1994, when I was selected to referee both tests between the All Blacks and France. The French had never won a test series out there and they had a very good side. The first test was in Christchurch and the second in Auckland. I was staying in the famous Avon Hotel and Berbizier asked if he could meet me for a coffee. I agreed and he came on his own. He's a very pleasant man and he explained how he wanted to play the game and what the strengths of his side were and how he wanted to win this series. He asked me what I wanted from his team. I told him straight away: "One word – discipline." I told him that I might make mistakes, and the teams may not even agree with my correct decisions. But I wanted all my decisions to be accepted. During the first test the French did just that. I could see they were biting their tongues on occasion but they accepted everything. It wasn't a very good game. New Zealand started questioning some of my decisions and I marched them back a few times. It was Jonah Lomu's first international and his lack of experience at the highest level showed, to the point that he was dropped for the second test. The French won the first test which gave them an enormous boost.

We moved up to Auckland for the next game. The All Blacks manager Colin Meads and coach Laurie Mains came to see me before the second test, and they were very annoyed that I was staying in the same hotel as the French team! But the New Zealand Rugby Union had booked all the accommodation. Meads and Mains felt that France had got away with a lot of offside in the first test and they wanted me to police this aspect a lot more closely. But that was their view. I'd seen a video of the game and was quite happy with the way it had gone. My touch judges were both Australians and had been okay with things as well.

Several thousand French supporters had arrived in Auckland because they could sniff the prospect of a test series victory. The ground was sold out and it was a massive game. The All Blacks really went for it straight from the kick off. Some of the rugby was phenomenal, it was a fantastic game. With about two minutes to go New Zealand were ahead by a few points and kicked the ball towards the French corner. Only France can gather the ball on their own line then send it through a dozen pairs of hands and score under the posts. It was magnificent to be standing there to award what was an outstanding try – it was a superb feeling, and one of the bonuses of being an international referee. The New Zealand players were trudging back, with their heads bowed because they were now losing after this wonder try. Sean Fitzpatrick looked up at me and I said "Wasn't that a brilliant try?" "Bollocks" was his reply. The conversion was good and France won. Perhaps my comment to Fitzpatrick was somewhat naïve. It was made on the spur of the moment: he gave me eye contact and I thought I had to say something. But perhaps he didn't like the grin on my face, either! The French were still out on the pitch twenty minutes after the final whistle. Every time I meet Pierre Berbizier he always says, "Discipline – I remember!"

A referee must have the respect of the players, without respect you won't succeed. There are times when players won't like your decisions either because you've made the wrong decision or they think you have. If they don't accept it they can be marched back ten metres. But it takes time to earn respect and a referee has to work at it. I have a sense of humour on the field but then you have to know when to use it. However, you can lighten a tense moment. There was an incident down in Whitland at one game in which I was trying to crack a joke with the players to defuse a situation. There were a couple of wags leaning on a fence watching the game. One of them said "Bevan isn't much of a referee is he?" The other replied "He's not much of a comedian either."

On the other hand, you have to keep a tight grip on some of the bully boys who exist in the game. You can't allow any player to rule the game just because he may be a 'character'. My main priority was discipline and which for me meant allowing the players to play the game. Players and coaches are looking to the referee to be consistent. There are some matches you have to take firm control in case it gets out of hand. Sometimes you have to blow the whistle early to keep players apart. In others you can stand back and just let them play. Ironically those are the games which get you noticed. You can work ten times harder in a match, to keep control, and have a much better game but you receive more criticism. One of my worst refereeing performances, if not *the* very worst was at the game between Pontypridd and Llanelli in the Cup in 1987. When I saw the video afterwards, I couldn't believe how badly I had refereed and how poor my touch judges had been. They felt that they had let me down. Both clubs were up for it: you could sense it in the dressing rooms. I let things go which I would normally act upon. I turned my back on certain incidents of foul play. Certain players were injured in off-the-ball incidents which the touch judges and I all missed. The game degenerated into an ugly, niggly farce. It affected both sides. Llanelli won but were incensed; after the game they just got straight on the coach and left immediately. Both clubs were disappointed with my refereeing and with the touch judges. I've asked myself many times how I allowed it to happen. Why didn't I sort them out? Why didn't I blow earlier?

It's unusual for all three officials to perform poorly. In fact I wasn't refereeing very well up to that game. I'd come back from the 1987 World Cup and maybe I wasn't giving each game the total concentration I should have. That was a lesson in itself. I don't think I was arrogant, I just didn't give it my all. The Pontypridd-Llanelli game came just before selection for the Five Nations and the WRU appointed Clive Norling and Les Peard. I'm certain I missed out because of my performance in that game.

My next game wasn't good either, it was a sort of hangover from the previous week. I really had to pull myself together. I was at a low and not enjoying this period in my refereeing career. I began blowing up early in the matches that followed in case things got out of hand. Word soon got around that I was losing my confidence. It was a big wake up call. Officials told me that they had seen me referee much better. Luckily I recognized what was happening, shook myself out of it and worked hard to get back on track, but it was the most miserable time of my career.

A referee must understand the game and understand what the players are trying to do. Referees are getting younger. Some decide as young as eighteen that they won't make it as a player and turn to refereeing. But knowing the laws isn't all there is to refereeing. If you apply the laws as they are written then you become more of a robot than a referee; you must have that feel for the game and that comes with experience, either as a player or with the whistle.

Fitness is an important part of modern refereeing. There is no argument: you have to be fit to do the job properly and today there is a tremendous emphasis on referee fitness. Referees must be able to keep up with the pace of the game, and the modern game requires a modern approach from the officials. More and more referees at international level are now full time professionals and have the time to dedicate themselves to extreme fitness. The English referees, for example, have a membership of a fitness club as part of their contract. This means that they can train every day of the week if necessary and their family life can revolve around that. I would say that most referees are doing gym work, aerobics, lifting weights for about two to three hours every day. My regime certainly wasn't that structured and my work commitments didn't allow me to put that amount of time into my fitness. I called in to a local gym on my way home from work Tuesdays and Thursdays and if I didn't happen to have a match on the weekend – which was rare – I might have gone for a run on a Saturday afternoon. Most of my exercise came through cycling, running and rowing on the machines in the gym.

Welsh referees have a fitness test once a year which involves the horrible 'bleep' test. It really is a lung buster. It involves shuttle runs back and forth to a 'beep' which gets progressively more frequent as the session goes on. Some people find it very, very difficult. The winger Ieuan Evans, I know, never managed to reach the mark which was set for the Lions. But Ieuan wasn't there to run back and forth. Ieuan was there to be given the ball and run in the tries. Referees must reach 11.5 on the 'bleep' test to be on the Welsh Premier panel, which is the top twelve. There is also a 3,000 metre run – which is seven and a half laps of the track which must be done in twelve and half minutes. That was set for the World Cup. On top of that there is a series of twenty and forty metre sprints done indoors and timed electronically. To qualify you must pass in all three sections. It's a fair old test.

I was never a great trainer as a player and if we did train twice a week with the Vardre then there was always a few pints afterwards as well. So all the good work in training was probably undone. The professional referees also have specialist treatment from dieticians and talk carbohydrate intake and so on. I've always been a good 'grubber' and I have never really gone in for any particular diet; I eat just as much junk food as good food. I've never been into that side of things. I know referees are supposed to be in tip top conditions and people say we shouldn't be drinking alcohol a week before a big game but I've never gone down that path. I've always enjoyed a pint on a Friday night but it has always been in moderation. Most of the modern referees will be teetotal for at least seventy-two hours before a big match. But this just adds to the pressures of a professional referee. I never wanted to be a 'professional' referee in the sense that it's my job. If you get to the stage where your hobby becomes your job then, for me, it loses something. If it's your job and it pays your mortgage then you're under pressure before you even step out onto the field. You must perform.

Some referees are earning £50,000 a year. In the southern hemisphere there is a fixed wage structure. English refs get a fixed fee plus a match fee. But what happens when a referee is making too many mistakes? All referees make errors but when you start making too many what happens? What do you do? If you're not being selected for matches you could be faced with a big cut in wages. In addition to the pressure that the coaches, the media, the big match atmosphere puts on you under, you now have to face the fact that your family is also depending on your performance out on the park. Then there are the assessors. Their decisions can also affect your salary. So I certainly I wouldn't have liked my livelihood to have depended on rugby.

You could argue that the modern game demands professional officials. But if we look back to the 1999 World Cup, the first one since the game went open, there were amateur officials alongside professional ones. If you consider the appointments, the professionals were no more successful than the amateurs. I define success in this instance by the appointments in the final stages, by criticism and assessors' marks. At international level, the assessors are from neutral countries; they provide a written report and give a mark on the referees' performance. Future fixtures depend on those marks.

I'm almost sure that assessors are amateurs. There are perks for them because they could be called upon to go anywhere in the world. So they either have a very good job or are retired. As a referee your future depends on them. There must be a system to evaluate and grade officials. A young lad with no experience can't be expected to referee Cardiff against Llanelli. It can't happen. Referees have to come through the grades and learn. There must be some sort of performance indicators.

The current system isn't perfect, though modern technology is increasingly playing a role. Assessors are now linked up to hear what the referee says during a game. So not only do the television and radio commentators hear what's going on, and sometimes the audience, even the crowds at the game, the assessors can also hear what the referee is telling the players. Some assessors want to hear what the touch judge is saying to the referee and we have the so-called 'talking flags'. The assessors now have a pretty informed idea of what officials are doing on the field. It is certainly a better thing for the referee.

One advantage, I suppose, in being a professional referee is the end of negotiations with your employer for time off to go to Argentina at the drop of a hat. Increasingly, employers are refusing permission. If you are a teacher for example, then you can't expect to go off to do a 'B' international in the south of France during term time. A referee has to be on location the day before the match these days. That sort of request can affect someone's career development if prospective employers think they may be let down. Co-workers may also be irritated by all the time off a colleague gets.

By becoming professional, the referee may fitter, healthier, and not have problems with an employer, but may suffer the stress that his livelihood depends upon his performance. Refereeing is in some ways easier now than it has ever been at the top level. First, there is the support of the touch judges with their talking flags to tell a referee what's going on behind him or that he's missed something obvious. There are numerous instances from the past where the technology would have saved everyone's blushes. In Wales we all remember the Irish try in Cardiff in 1989. The referee, Roger Quittenton, missed a blatant knock on by an Irish player who half stopped himself and then almost embarressedly picked up the ball and scored under the posts. Of course, the crowd went mad but the referee hadn't seen it and Ireland won 19-13. That kind of situation could never arise now. The touch judge could now speak into his flag and tell the referee, "Knock-on green, scrum down red ball".

The new technology allows the officials to work together better as a team. My philosophy was if I didn't signal touch judges should assume that I hadn't seen something, even if it was obvious. If I'd seen an infringement I would hold out my arm to show the players and crowd that I was allowing advantage, but also a signal to the touch judges that there was no need for them to rabbit in my ear!

The flags are a big help particularly for off-the-ball incidents or foul play, especially on the blind side of a ruck or maul. I had my doubts when they were first introduced as you do with some laws. But they have proved extremely useful, and will be even more so after some redesign. Often they only work for 75 to 80 per cent of the time. In my final international between Ireland and Italy they didn't work for the whole of the first half. So we had to revert to hand signals. Some of the flag designs are voice-activated and miss the first few words which are spoken. During 1999 World Cup, when Canada played France the officials had a crazy system of communication. They had decided that if the ball was grounded properly over the tryline the touch judge would shout 'TRY' and if it wasn't he would shout out 'NO TRY', just for decisions in the corner. But there was a slight delay after the button on the flag was pressed, so the touch judge spoke too soon. The referee didn't hear his 'NO', only the 'TRY' and gave it! The television commentator was horrified. The player had clearly lost the ball over the line but was still awarded the try on the misheard call of the touch judge. You couldn't really blame the touch judge – perhaps he was over-enthusiastic in his use of the button. All the officials got together after that incident and now use a straightforward and non-confusing "YES" or "NO". Further technology in the form of a video referee could have reversed the decision, of course. I'm sure modern technology can come up with a system where a microphone is pinned to the jersey and provides open and continuous communication.

At the end of the day it's the referee's call. A touch judge can only give advice through the flag. As a referee you can either take that advice or ignore it. I would tell my touch judges not to be upset if I over-ruled them because I might have seen something which they had not. Or it might have been too fine a call, just inches over the offside line for example, and I've decided to let it go. You rise or fall by your own decisions. I'm not being hard on touch judges but the referee is solely responsible out in the middle, so while it's always good to get advice it doesn't have to be taken. In the case of the touch judge in that France-Canada game, he wasn't going to stand and argue with the referee. It was up to the referee to listen or not. The touch judge might have thought that the referee was in a better position and had seen it differently.

The same conditions stand for foul play. I was never in a situation to use video referees. One of their drawbacks is the slowness in communicating decisions. There's a lot of hanging around and if it's cold and wet it can have an adverse effect on the players. And some referees are asking for the video referee for guidance on obvious calls, and are shying away from making the decision. It's much better to get on with the game. In some ways the talking flags can help out much more effectively. In cricket, decisions on run-outs are easier to make by video review. But when you are dealing with sixteen bodies in a ruck or maul driving over the line it's almost impossible for a video referee to rule and there can be a three or four minute wait whilst he studies it from different angles and still have no decision – or the wrong one – at the end of it. The referee then has to opt for his original decision and go for a scrum five. Video has its good points. If an incident occurs in open play then one of the three officials should have seen it. If it's in a ruck or a maul then it's going to be difficult for the camera to see anything.

The pace of technological change and the ends for which it is used has been swift. When we first wore microphones it was for the benefit of the commentators, to help them understand what was going on and to pass information on to the viewers or listeners. There was no way we wanted the audience to hear directly what we were saying. On occasions we may have had to use some strong language to get a point over to a player. It was difficult for some referees to curb their language. One in particular was reprimanded at the Gnoll in Neath for bad language which was heard by television viewers. The rugby pitch is like working underground, you're in the middle of an all male situation; sometimes you had to tell a player in no uncertain terms exactly where he stood, and there was only one way of doing that. So we were very wary about microphones at the beginning and the media companies had to assure us that we would only be heard by the commentators. Then in South Africa it was decided that the audience would benefit from hearing what the referee told the players. In some matches the crowd could also listen via the public address system! That's absolutely crazy.

People tell me that they turn the sound down on their televisions for some matches because the referee's constant talking gets on their nerves. They get fed up and I agree with them. Why should the referee have to tell a scrum half on every occasion, 'down the middle'? He knows that. Why should you have to tell the back row to stay down at a scrum when they've lost the ball? Some referees must have sore throats by the end of a game because the instruction is non-stop. What right has the referee to say 'get away reds' to a defending side? They have as much right to compete for the ball as the attacking side. Both sides have an opportunity to compete for the ball and I don't think that some teams are getting it. Things are stacked in favour of the attacking side and referees are telling players to 'get back' or 'leave them have it' just to make life easier on themselves. You can also get on players' nerves. Some players will say to you, 'talk to me ref'. But why? Why should the officials have to talk all the time? We've brought the problem on ourselves. We don't get quick ball because a man is tackled and goes to ground, and he won't let go until the referee tells him to! He should let the ball go immediately, but because players are so used to referees rabbitting on at them they are waiting for his instruction to release the ball or roll away from the tackled player. So perhaps it's the referees fault for slowing down what should be quick ball in the modern game.

Referees also have Citing Commissioners now, introduced during the 1999 World Cup, to deal with foul play. They have a television screen and the facilities to see different angles of an incident. If all three on-pitch officials miss an act of foul play the commissioner can bring a player to task. Before the World Cup if I had seen an act of foul play and deemed it a yellow card offence or just a penalty then the player could not be cited, because I had dealt out the punishment on the pitch. During the World Cup I could give a yellow card for trampling. But the commissioner could deem it a red card offence, and a committee would be set up to deal with the offending player. Some referees believe that this process undermines their authority on the field. But referees *do* make mistakes. An incident might be far more serious than first thought when it is viewed from a different angle. It's always good to confer with a touch judge but the referee still might have been the only official to have seen it. If the citing commissioner upholds your view then it can only be a positive thing. Ultimately, what we want are the correct decisions on the laws of the game but also on foul play.

There is far more onus on players to behave in the modern game. A professional player is hit in the pocket if he is guilty of foul play – not only from a possible fine but because he'll miss out on future match fees and lose wages. If a player is suspended for a month then he's no good to his club for that period of time. Having said that, it never entered my mind that a player might lose money if I sent him off. That consideration shouldn't interfere with a referee's decisions. It's the player's own responsibility. If I was a professional referee and a particular player warranted sending off then my livelihood would be affected if I didn't make the right decision. I believe that I'm correct in saying that most players don't give a damn about a referee's career. Not one iota. So a referee looks after himself and the laws of the game.

As television coverage of rugby developed, any mistakes became more obvious – and to a much wider audience. I would have butterflies in my stomach when I watched videos of my matches to see if all my decisions had been correct. I paid particular attention to any decisions which had been queried by players during the game. Normally I found it difficult to watch a recording of myself on television. I usually watched a game twice. The first time I looked at my own performance: was my positioning on the field right, was I up with play, was I taking too many short cuts? The second time I could relax and enjoy the game.

I believe that it is fair in this professional era for the performance of the referee to be open to scrutiny. Players themselves come under the microscope and every missed tackle is seized upon. Refereeing has never been easier at international level because there is so much help and support. But there's a lot of pressure too, which has increased because there's now so much at stake. Referees are quick enough to accept the £1,500 fee for an international or £750 for running touch. Like any other job, though, if you don't perform then you'll suffer. I believe that supporters have a right to moan about the performance of players and equally they can moan about the referee if he's not performing well.

The best law in the book is undoubtedly the advantage law. You cannot coach the advantage law to anybody. You can instruct or advise but no two referees apply the advantage law in the same way, it is all down to interpretation. As a result there are often complaints about a referee giving a team two bites of a cherry. The law itself is quite clear. Advantage should be immediate and can either be possessional or territorial. The frequent case is the ball from the scrum half to the outside half at the set play from which a drop at goal is attempted and the defending side have encroached offside. If the kick succeeds the attacking side gets three points because advantage has been played. But then if it fails, the referee shouldn't take play back and give the attackers a penalty. The advantage was the opportunity to kick for three points. Bringing play back is the second bite of the cherry.

The referee should be consistent. He shouldn't allow different lengths of advantage. There shouldn't be a longer advantage if a team is attacking in the opponents' twenty two than if they were defending on the half way line. Although it's the best law in the book it's also the one least consistently refereed. Advantage in Scotland in my earlier days would be allowed to continue for quite a while – to a farcical point. Players would say that if they had a Scottish referee the game would flow!

Thankfully bad laws have been weeded out, such as penalties for minor offences like crooked feed or foot up, which could be awarded at the whim of a referee. Certainly those offences weren't worth potentially losing three points. Instead there is the differential penalty for which the referee can give free kicks instead.

I would also like to see a new law introduced of a ten metres offside line for the backs from a scrum. It would be easy to police: the touch judges could do it as they do at a line out. Obviously it couldn't be done at rucks and mauls. At the set scrum the law already exists where the back rows must stay down and the scrum half must stay in close proximity to his opponent, so outside halves have never had it so good for space. If we could bring in a law where the offside line is ten metres back from the centre of the scrum then there would be a twenty metres gap between opposing sets of backs. I believe that this would lead to more exciting play from set-pieces, but conversely would be an absolute dream for the drop kick specialists. I would like to see the drop goal banished. Certainly I don't think it's worth three points. So if we change the laws to give more freedom to the outside half then I would certainly like to see the drop kick diminished in value.

It seems strange for a former flanker to be advocating more space for the outside half. I usually got to the opposing outside half once and gave away a penalty! On one occasion the Vardre were playing against Llandybie in a Cup game. They had a very talented outside half called Gwyn Ashby who had run rings around us earlier in the season. So the order went out for me to put one in early on. Irrespective of what he would do, he was going to have one! So I did exactly that and it was going to be late and painful. It's an awful thing to say but it was our way of counteracting skill! He kicked ahead and I got him. It was a tremendous midriff challenge and I heard the wind surging out from him. He'd been hurt. The referee was the late Denzil Lloyd from Nantyffyllon who was on the international panel. Like all experienced referees he didn't follow the kick but glanced behind him and caught me in the act. He made sure that Ashby was okay and came for me. He told me that he knew exactly what I was doing and gave me a final warning. This meant that I had to tread very carefully for the remaining seventy-five minutes. Ashby could either be lacking in bravery and keep one eye out for me which meant I would have won our little game within a game. But he did the exact opposite and made a complete fool of me for the rest of the game. He dummied me, went around me when he pleased with his superior pace. Once he held out the ball and taunted me. Like an idiot I went for it but he then danced around me and I could hear the laughter from the Llandybie supporters. The truth is that the first time I touched him was when I'd hit him late and the second time that I'd touched him was to shake his hand after the game. I'd brought it on myself.

My hero was Terry Cobner. He was leading the Pontypool pack, for which I had a tremendous respect. Early in my career in the top flight, when I was given a fixture between Pontypool and Bristol on a Tuesday night I really hoped that Cobner would be playing. I had never refereed at Pontypool Park before. Mike Rafter, the England flanker was the Bristol captain. I called the two skippers out before the game and shook their hands. 'Cob' wished me all the best and welcomed me to Pontypool. He was calling me 'Sir' during the game. If I had to sort one of his players out he told me "Leave it to me Sir". I though that this was great. He was doing my work for me. At the end of the match which Pontypool won and 'Cob' shook my hand after the game and thanked me. He told me there'd always be a welcome in Pontypool for people like me. I thought that this was a great day and that I had obviously performed well. Rafter then came on to me. He also thanked me and said "I'm going to thank the other referee now – Terry Cobner." In the clubhouse afterwards Rafter came up to me once again and said "I hope you didn't mind me saying that at the end of the game?" "Not at all," I replied, "I can take a joke". "But I wasn't joking," he said. "I was very serious. Almost every fifty-fifty situation you gave it to them." Cobner had been so clever, he'd worked me a treat. The next time I went to Pontypool, Cobner started the same thing again. But this time I turned to him and said "When I want your help skipper, I'll ask for it". Cobner grinned. He'd been tumbled, the boy referee had grown up.

Back with the laws, there's also the issue of the mark and the free kick allowed for it. Although it is the last line of defence, it has been made easier for the defending player because the mark can be called from three feet in the air. The attacking side can't make a similar call so it is a law exclusively favouring the defending side. That isn't consistent because of the advantage for one player in a man to man situation. Changing the law might lead to more up-and-unders because the defender wouldn't have the cushion of the mark – but what's wrong with a good up-and-under? It would be a great test of character for the defender and would encourage his own team to get back to support him. But it has to be a good up-and-under; a poor one gives the defending side an opportunity to counter attack, because the attackers are kicking away possession.

International referees are getting younger and younger. I was amazed out in New Zealand to find sixteen- and seventeen-year olds refereeing at senior schoolboy level. They had decided that their career was going to be in refereeing not as a player. Stuart Dickinson of Australia is in his early thirties and has already refereed international matches for several years. But do these young referees really know what the players are trying to do if they haven't played the game? As I've already said, there are plenty of aids for the referee in the modern game, so maybe it isn't as important as it used to be that you must have played the game. A lot of the referees around at the moment would have finished their playing career much earlier and turned to refereeing with the benefit of hindsight. If you play rugby until you're thirty-three or thirty-four, then you won't make it to the top in Welsh refereeing. I wouldn't have done it. An injury stopped me from playing; if I had gone back to playing I certainly wouldn't have made it as far as I have done as a referee.

I've been very impressed with Stuart Dickinson on the occasions that I've seen him. I've run touch for Steve Walsh from New Zealand and expect great things from him. Paddy O'Brien is also high on my list. He didn't have the greatest of World Cups – he was disappointed with his own performance and suffered as a result. Colin Hawke from New Zealand got some bad press too, not all warranted by any means and, like O'Brien, missed out. In Europe there are high hopes for Nigel Whitehouse of Wales. He's another poacher turned gamekeeper and one of the few referees who played first class rugby, for South Wales Police and Llanelli. England's Chris White is also a star of the future. There's a young lad called Jonathan Kaplan who did very well when he refereed Italy's victory over Scotland in the first Six Nations.

Those are the top referees for the coming years. They've come up the hard way and now enjoy the new structures at international level, the fourth and sometimes fifth official sorting out the replacements and the blood bins, and all the other things I've mentioned. But the hardest refereeing is in the lower divisions where the referee is on his own. He's got to keep the score, deal with the sin-bins, the blood bins, the replacements, without any help from the touch judges. He's often still got two committeemen running touch and he's also got to have eyes in the back of his head. Officiating at this level is still a great experience for premier league and international referees because it brings you back down to earth. It reminds you that you can become lazy and that you have to have your wits about you. So all the modern paraphernalia is for a lucky few. The Vardre will never have a video referee or a citing commissioner! Assessors do get around and assessment in Wales goes all the way down to Division Seven. The ideal situation would be to assess everyone every Saturday. But what referees need at the local level are coaches who can work with them to build on their strengths. I believe you should be assessed at international and Premier level but the others should be coached. They should be told which areas of their game to improve on and be checked by the coach after a month's time to see if that referee has progressed. A coach could have half a dozen referees under his wing as a mentor.

I don't know if I'd be any good at that. I have to be involved in the game in some shape or form. You don't just throw twenty-eight years of rugby away like that, but I'm employed as a trainer of apprentices with BP so would I also enjoy doing it as a hobby? I don't think I owe the game anything in that I've earned everything I've done in it. I've worked hard on my fitness, and on my faults and weaknesses. I've been fortunate to travel all over the world, stay in fabulous hotels and eat at the finest restaurants. No doubt some people would feel that I *do* owe the game something, after all only a small percentage of referees become internationals. But maybe I owe Welsh referees something, and if I can help them then I will. I'm already doing that to an extent now, unofficially. I get phone calls from young referees during the week asking for advice about something or other. I hope that I've been able to help young referees who are reticent in speaking out in case they are marked down.

In recent years we've seen the beginnings of women referees, who have been officiating at schoolboy level, particularly in the Cardiff area. This is a development to be encouraged if we are to have properly trained and experienced women's referees for women's fixtures. I don't know whether women will ever referee men's fixtures at a low level or beyond. The men's game is very physical and steeped in a male culture which perhaps wouldn't welcome an official from the opposite sex. Men must continue to referee the women's matches at the moment because there aren't enough women to do it. I refereed a women's international at the

National Stadium between Wales and England and found it a different experience. Although I didn't know what to expect, I took my role very seriously because it was clearly such an important occasion for the players.

The World Cup Years – 1987

The lead-in to the first World Cup in Australia and New Zealand in 1987 had begun for me a year previously when I visited New Zealand for the first time in 1986. I love going to New Zealand, I've refereed there more often than any other country. New Zealanders are wonderful people and give you a tremendous welcome. Nowadays things have changed somewhat because you're there to do a job and left more to your own devices. Whereas during the amateur days Referees' Society members were much keener to mix with you socially. Professional referees are treated differently because now it's their occupation. On my arrival in 1986, I hit it off straight away with a guy called John Cormick who was President of the Bay of Plenty Referees and we've been close friends ever since. He showed me all over the area around Rotorua, which is a magnificent place. There was no subsistence allowance so we were hosted everywhere and were completely spoilt: there was always someone who wanted to take you out to dinner, or boating, or shark fishing. The itinerary was a full one.

As a warm up to the tests between New Zealand and Australia, my first game was between the Bay of Plenty and Auckland. Auckland were the national champions and full of All Blacks, including their captain Andy Haden and the Whetton brothers. Earlier in the season I had refereed Pontypool at Newbridge in front of a packed crowd and I had sent off Kevin Moseley, the Pontypool (later Wales) second row. After checking the studs of he Auckland players I then went into the Bay of Plenty dressing room. The first thing I heard was a Welsh voice saying "Oh shit, it's Bevan!" Who was standing in the corner but Kevin Moseley, ready to play for Bay of Plenty. His discipline was excellent and he gave a very good account of himself jumping against Andy Haden.

I had been appointed to referee the first two tests of the three test series. The first was in Athletic Park, Wellington, the second in Carisbrook, Dunedin. Brian Lochore was the manager/coach of the All Blacks and Alan Jones coached Australia. I really built myself up for the first Test, though there was an incident in which I was completely wiped out. I became caught up in a ruck and enveloped. Luckily, I managed to blow my whistle from the bottom of the pile! But the game went exceptionally well. Australia won 13-12 and there were no complaints from either side. Even the press were complimentary of my performance.

For the next fortnight, everywhere I went, everyone kept telling me how well I had done in the first Test and all of this went to my head completely. Because the All Blacks had lost they were considering selecting the 'Rebels' who had gone on the controversial South Africa tour. The rugby public in New Zealand was split over the issue, but the selectors went ahead and chose some of the rebels. There was nonetheless a full house at Carisbrook. Following all the compliments and good press I believed by now that I was a far better referee than I actually was. I went on to the field in the second Test with the wrong attitude. My game was lethargic; I was continually caught out of position; I wasn't concentrating and wasn't clamping down on the things I should have done. It culminated in my missing a try for the Australian number eight, Steve Tuynman, through bad positioning. When you disallow a try, you can normally tell from the players reaction how disappointed he is. Some will try to con you, but Tuynman looked genuinely disappointed because the game was on a knife edge. I gave a scrum five, because I wasn't really able to see it, and this time the All Blacks won the game 13-12. So the 'try' which I had not awarded had a bearing on the outcome. Tom Doocey from New Zealand, was one of my touch judges and told me bluntly that I had missed a try. We didn't have talking flags then and referees didn't really take much notice of the touch judges apart from the bread and butter of lineouts, penalties and conversions.

So I was the villain, especially in the eyes of the Australians. Alan

Jones wasted no time in going to the Press and absolutely slating me. I got a real blasting and it was very personal. When I got to the post-match reception they were showing a rerun of the match. When it came to the 'try' incident it was far from convincing from the main camera. This was some relief to me. From the reverse camera angle you still couldn't call it. I thought that I might have got away with it. But when the roving touchline camera angle was shown, it was obvious. I could see myself in the wrong position, still in my dream world, and I had missed it. All the eyes in the reception turned to look at me and at that moment I just wanted the ground to open up and swallow me. It had cost Australia victory and had drawn the series.

Their captain, Andy Slack, presented me with their customary tie, and without being impolite, but the look on his face spoke louder than strong words. No-one would talk to me. I was clutching at straws. I wanted an Australian, somewhere, to forgive me, but they didn't say a word to me. If they had called me names, I would have been relieved. But here was a stone-cold silence. Every time I tried to make polite conversation I was ignored. I went to the toilet and there was the Australian prop, Rodriguez. He checked to make sure there was nobody in the cubicles before he said anything. Then he told me that the Australian team had been instructed not to bother with me at all. What a lesson to learn. I vowed then that I would never, ever go out onto any field with the same attitude again. The Press the following day were full of complaints, condemning my inept performance. And they say a week is a long time in politics; a fortnight earlier the very same people who were now castigating me had been heaping praise on me.

On reflection, it was the worst performance out of all my forty four internationals. I had never felt so low after a game and it was a relief that within two days I was flying home. As it was the middle of summer in Wales I thought I could have a break from it all. But it didn't stop when I left New Zealand. The *South Wales Evening Post* had picked up the story and all my mates at home knew about it. I actually brought some of the press articles back with me so that they would bring me back down to earth whenever I got cocky. Thankfully, Australia won the third test and claimed the series.

Prior to the World Cup the Welsh Referees Committee had told us that each of the IRB countries – apart from South Africa who were still banned – would have two officials at the tournament. Australia and New Zealand as the hosts would also supply extra touch judges for games which didn't involve either country. We were all waiting with baited breath to find out who would be chosen. I received the long-awaited phone call from Denzil Lloyd, Chairman of the Welsh Referees, to inform me that I had been selected along with Clive. It was congratulations all round and the phone didn't stop ringing.

I had been hopeful. Realistically, it had been a choice of two out of three, Clive, myself and Winston. Unfortunately, on this occasion, Winston missed out. My elation was tempered with a great deal of sadness for him. He had been a great mentor to me, and with four years between World Cups, this was his only chance before retirement. Clive celebrated with his curly perm and really looked the part of an international referee! We teased him in New Zealand that he looked like a white Tongan!

The two English referees were to be Fred Howard and Roger Quittenton. I'd not really come across Roger until then though he was one of the senior officials in world rugby. Brian Anderson and Jim Fleming were selected from Scotland, and Stephen Hilditch and Dave Burnett from Ireland. Jim and I were the two youngsters. We Welsh referees were told we would travel out with the referees from Ireland, England and Scotland, and that we would be sharing the same flight as the Welsh and Scottish teams.

It was a horrendous trip. We were all in economy and had to make our own fun. There would be two breaks on the way. We were on Air New Zealand from Gatwick to Los Angeles where we stopped for three hours. With four or five nationalities thrown together on the flight the banter and mickey-taking was flowing thick and fast. Mick Doyle, the Irish coach, was the only one who had American dollars so he held court in the airport bar. The next thing we saw was this chap whizzing past us in a tracksuit. We weren't sure who it was until he went past us again and we saw it was Roger Quittenton doing his sprinting practice. He's a fitness fanatic, and quite an extrovert. Then it was on to Hawaii and a further two hours break before the final leg to Auckland. As we were about to land the pilot informed us that the famous Auckland fog had rolled in and we were to circle for half an hour to wait for it to clear. But it didn't clear and we were diverted to Christchurch, on the South Island. Christchurch, then, was not an international airport, so there were no customs. No-one was allowed to get off the plane and we had another three hour wait. We were all very tired and hungry, and after such a long flight all the supplies on board were depleted. But the airline couldn't open the doors because of pest control procedures. Eventually we took off and went back to Auckland, where our liaison officers were still waiting for us five hours after we were due to arrive.

It was mid-afternoon by this time and they suggested we watch a game at Eden Park. But the first thing Roger wanted to do was to go training instead. Already, he was setting himself apart from the rest of us, but total dedication to his own routine was his way of life. So while we went off to Eden Park to watch a game of rugby and enjoy a few drinks with our hosts, Roger went on a different bus to do his own thing. Unfortunately, when he arrived at the hotel he found his training kit was on our bus at Eden Park!

There was more to come between Roger and myself. At breakfast at the hotel on the first morning, Roger was eating a delicious-looking muesli. I couldn't see it anywhere in the buffet so I had to ask where he had it from. He told me it was his own special concoction that he had brought over from England with him, and that he couldn't possibly give me any because he had measured out only enough for himself for the whole tournament! Once again his meticulous planning was coming to the fore.

We were given our kit, and we already knew what our fixtures were for the early rounds. My first game was running the line for Clive in the Tonga-Canada match in Hawke's Bay. My first game in the middle would be New Zealand versus Fiji in Christchurch. It was notable for one reason. By this time Fiji had more or less qualified and rested their star players to give all the other players in the squad a game. Not surprisingly, the All Blacks won convincingly, it was a stroll for them. When a game is so one-sided there are very few talking points. My second one in the middle, up in Auckland, proved to be a similar affair between France and Zimbabwe. Because France wanted to top their group they fielded a strong side, and Camberabero scored a record number of points.

Like the teams, the referees also knew that not all of us would make it through to the knockout stages. If you weren't selected to go on then you would be on the flight home: the organisers didn't require all the referees for the whole tournament. There was no structured, official assessment system in operation so the decision rested on the views of the tournament administrators. The way we were informed was dreadful. There were bad evenings, with a lot of ill-feeling, in both the 1987 and 1991 World Cups.

The referees were told the evening after the quarter final stages. I'd been officiating in Auckland in the France vs Fiji match. It was a fabulous game of rugby, Roger and I were running touch for Clive with Fred Howard as number four official. On one occasion Roger and I were behind the posts as France took a penalty. We had both been to New Zealand before and the crowd behind the posts were quite close to the pitch. The Kiwis were neutrals in this game and were enjoying themselves. We heard someone shout out "Touch judge, you're a wanker!" Roger told me: "Ignore them Derek". I responded, "But they're not talking to me Roger, they're talking to you." I even got a smile out of him. Clive handled the game very well. France won it 31-16 but it could have gone either way.

I didn't think Clive was a hundred per cent fit. He'd had an ankle injury which had prevented him from running touch for me at Christchurch in the New Zealand game and he probably wasn't completely over it. But he was probably the only referee in the world who could give such an impressive performance in the middle whilst carrying an injury. You couldn't decide afterwards whether to plant carrots or potatoes in the furrow he'd ploughed up and down the middle of the pitch! That evening, I told Clive I though his performance would mean his selection for the latter stages. But he had his doubts. It certainly wasn't Roger's day. During our meal that night the waiter came to our table with a bottle of white wine and a bottle of red wine balanced on a tray. I opted for the white wine and when the waiter took the bottle off his tray the red tipped all over Roger!

The following night we were eating in the hotel restaurant on the harbour in Auckland. We had decided to treat ourselves and were enjoying a fine meal when there was a call for Fred Howard to go to reception. When Fred returned ten minutes later he was very pale, almost white. He'd looked as if he'd seen a ghost. Roger asked him what was wrong. Fred said he'd taken a phone call was from the New Zealand Rugby Union and they'd given him the future appointments. We thought it was a very strange way to let us know. Roger asked Fred eagerly what the appointments were. Fred looked at me and said "In two days time, Bev, you're flying to Sydney to run touch in the semifinal between France and Australia, the referee is Brian Anderson and the second touch judge is Jim Fleming. I'm off to Brisbane to run touch in the semi between Wales and New Zealand and the referee is Kerry Fitzgerald. I'm sorry to tell you, Roger and Clive, that you're on the next flight home."

It was completely unfair that Fred had to tell us and, of course, the evening died a death. Clive, although disappointed, felt it had been coming. I was shocked for him because of his display in the quarter final. Roger was devastated and went off to his room. The officials for the final were told in the same way, when I was informed I was going to be the fourth official. It was another phone call and this time Jim Fleming was the unfortunate one to take it. Kerry Fitzgerald was surprised to be in the middle because he'd just done a semifinal and thought that would be it for him. We let our feelings be known quite strongly at the end of the tournament.

There was some humour, too. A day after the semis phone call, when Roger had got over his disappointment, I did ask him if I could now have the rest of his muesli because he wouldn't be needing it. His answer is unprintable. We'd miss Roger, in a way. I'd heard stories about him previously, how he liked to get to a game ridiculously early – which he did! Fred and I ran touch for him in the Italy-Argentina pool match in Christchurch. He was a man set on his procedures who had a complete, planned structure to which he adhered at all times. The talk with the captains had to be at a certain time, as did checking the studs and the toss of the coin. Then he wanted twenty minutes alone in the dressing room. So Fred and I then had to go for a walk. Then he would give us full instruction of what he required from us as touch judges, including smiling if things went well. (He didn't tell us what he wanted us to do if things went badly.) The previous day he'd run touch for me in the pool game between New Zealand and Fiji. Clive had pulled out with his ankle injury, so Roger was asked to do it. Originally he refused because it totally upset all his preparations for the following day. The organisers then ordered him to do it but wasn't happy at all.

Fred Howard started as the junior of the two English referees but he had a tremendous tournament and he was rewarded with the third place play-off between Wales and Australia, that famous game in Rotorua. I thought Fred was unlucky not to be given the final. I was in the stand at Rotorua watching with the Australian Kerry Fitzgerald who would be taking charge of the final. Wales had been humbled by New Zealand in the semifinal and were determined to win back some pride. Apart from the result a major talking point was Fred's sending off of Australia's David Cody after an earlier warning. Kerry was very quiet because Cody was a personal friend.

That evening the teams and the officials had their own dinner whilst the rest of us were hosted by the Bay of Plenty Referees Society where they would join up with us later. When we all got together I congratulated Fred on an excellent game – particularly from the Welsh perspective. I asked him how the function afterwards had gone and Fred replied. "It was strange", he said, "none of the Australians spoke to me after the game." I knew exactly how he felt!

Ironically after returning from the World Cup, I received a phone call inviting me to referee the Bledisloe Cup match between Australia and New Zealand in Sydney. This was to be New Zealand's first test match as World Champions. I explained the situation to Denzil Lloyd who told me it was thought, at the time, I was the best one for the job. Clive was bitterly disappointed because he wanted to show them that he was a first-class referee and the organisers had been wrong to send him home early from the World Cup. And he would have done so. I felt the one who really should have had the game was Winston, as Clive and I had gone to the World Cup. I made my feelings known, but there was no guarantee that if I didn't go that another Welshman would. I had to go back to my employers, BP, to ask for some more time off after just returning from five weeks away. They were so good about it they even asked me to do some work for BP in Singapore on the way home.

The game was a classic. This was Brian Lochore's last game before stepping down as manager/coach of New Zealand. They wanted him to retire with both the World Cup and Bledisloe Cup, so they played for Brian. Joe Stanley, the All Blacks centre, had a huge game. He was well known for getting so psyched up before a game that he was sick at some stage of the match. And true to form he did exactly that – in glorious technicolour – right in front of me. He was also voted man of the match. The game ended 16-30 to New Zealand. My touch judges were Bob Fordham and Kerry Fitzgerald and it couldn't have gone better. It was such a relief because the Australian press had been reminding everyone about my performance the previous year. This time the Australians were speaking to me! They had regained some pride because finishing fourth behind Wales had been a major blow for them.

The World Cup Years – 1991

The 1991 World Cup retained the 1987 format, with each country selecting two referees. In Wales, there were again probably three of us going for the two positions: this time it was Clive Norling, Les Peard and myself. Of course, each one of us was doing our best to impress and things became quite competitive. I had only refereed five international matches in the years since the 1987 World Cup: Australia vs New Zealand in 1987, Ireland vs Fiji & Western Samoa in 1988, New Zealand vs Scotland in 1990 and Ireland vs France in 1991. I was still in the early stages of my international career and I suppose whenever a tough appointment had to be made, it went to Clive. He was the proven man, but at that particular time there were changes on the referees' panel, Denzil Lloyd was the Chairman of the Referees Committee and Ken Rowlands had just been appointed the first full time Director of Referees in Wales. On the field, Les had also come into contention.

I felt my chances were better than even with two out of three to be chosen. And since Wales were making the selection of their own referees, form at home was far more significant than how you performed away in international matches, so perhaps only having had charge of five wasn't a factor. There was still that amount of bitterness from Clive because he felt that he had been stabbed in the back at the last World Cup and he'd been annoyed by being overlooked for the Bledisloe match shortly afterwards. The rivalry was certainly there. We all had our different styles of refereeing. Clive was flamboyant. Les was very efficient, he knew his stuff and was very much a player's referee.

That particular year, the semifinals of the Welsh Cup were held at the old National Stadium. Clive and I were to do the semis and Les, the final, so we all had the chance to referee a big game on the big stage. In the final, Les put Mark Jones of Neath in the sin-bin for stamping, the first time the sin-bin had been used. I must admit that I am in favour of the sin-bin despite the criticism that some referees use it as a soft option. Eventually the wait for the World Cup was over. The letter came that Les and myself had been chosen and Clive had missed out. It was another major disappointment for Clive, and I felt that this was the end for him as a referee. I think it hurt him far more than he was prepared to tell people. He took up an offer of a position on the ITV commentary team covering the tournament, but because he was still a member of the Welsh Referees' Society and an active referee it was difficult for him to criticize anybody.

The English representatives were Ed Morrison and Fred Howard who was already being tipped for the final. He was refereeing superbly. New Zealand had David Bishop and Keith Lawrence, France had Patrick Robin and René Hourquet, Ireland had Steve Hilditch and Owen Doyle, Scotland had the same two-Brian Anderson and Jim Fleming, Australia had Sandy Macneil and Kerry Fitzgerald. Once again there were no representatives from South Africa. But this time we had referees from the emerging rugby nations such as Zimbabwe, Romania, the United States and Japan. Everyone was to be based in Cardiff. Our kit was supplied by Cotton Traders and the expenses were bed and breakfast plus laundry and £50 per day. Ken Rowlands took charge of the referees' finances and on our first pay day we received fourteen days' allowances which we had to check and sign for. When the Romanian referee was given his envelope he couldn't quite believe it. The previous night we had shared a beer and he had explained that he was having great difficulty in phoning home. At the time the country was controlled by Ceaucescu and when this particular referee managed to speak with his wife on the telephone, he could hear gunfire in the background. He was a worried man, but here he was in Cardiff to referee in a World Cup. When he checked his allowances his face went white. He must have counted the money three or four times. He asked me, "Is this all for me?" I told him it was and that there'd be more to come. He said, "At home I could buy an apartment with this!" He was a wealthy man because of his referees' allowances!

There was to be a referees' cut again with most of those going from the emerging nations; but undoubtedly there would be one or two familiar names going with them. The man in charge of the referees was the late Peter Brooke of England. He was outstanding. The referees were supported in a much better way in this tournament. If there were problems with logistics, like transport, they were quickly sorted out. Brooke had our best interests at heart. If there were mistakes made he would take us to one side and tell us that he'd apologised on our behalf and to let things rest.

There was also an assessment system operating in 1991 and the way it was used was a major improvement on the situation in 1987. I went to Beziers in France with Les and the Japanese referee, Yagi-San, as we called him. We had all been given a referee to mentor from the emerging nations and Yagi and I were paired up as buddies. We arrived in our hotel to find a terrible dump. The water from the taps was brown and the room was tacky. It was dreadful. Les was staying just down the corridor and I shouted down to him. "Isn't this a dive? They promised us the best and look at the hole they've put us in. I bet you won't find the IRB staying in an hotel like this!" Keith Rowlands was the Secretary of the IRB at the time and I heard his voice right behind me. "Any problems Derek?" he said. "None at all," I replied, "quaint little hotel isn't it?" We discovered later that it was the only hotel which hadn't been checked out beforehand.

Les was to referee France vs Romania and Yagi-San and I were to run touch. It was an evening game. Yagi was an outstanding character. Our kit was large or extra large. Yagi was a very small Japanese gentleman. People must have wondered why there were roars of laughter coming from the referees' changing room. Yagi's socks were touching his shorts and he was stuffing paper into his boots, which were about three sizes to big for him. He was such a lovely chap he just wore what he was given, he wouldn't complain at all. His socks had to be rolled back half a dozen times before they fitted.

When it came to the game itself we had to work out what we would do, as touch judges, when we were behind the posts for a kick at goal. So I told him that we would take a post each and shout 'YES' if the kick was over or 'NO' if it wasn't, and the shout would have to be loud to be heard over the noise of the crowd. "Okay Bevan-San," was his reply. When it came for the first kick at goal, the ball went towards Yagi's side. He just looked across and put his flag up straightaway and ran back to his touch line. I told Les to tell him once again to shout 'Yes' or 'No'. The next kick came on my side and I shouted "YES" very loudly to make the point to Yagi. We both came behind the posts for the third kick at goal and I reminded him again: "You must shout Yagi, 'YES' or 'NO'." The kick was a very tight one and was on Yagi's side. He looked at me, and I looked at him and he shouted "I THINK SO!" And up went his flag. I was a nervous wreck. Whenever there were kicks at goal I prayed they would come to my side. Fortunately the match wasn't in doubt and France were comfortable winners, otherwise it could have been very awkward indeed. Neither was it a very good game. We'd been given a directive about players diving in at the tackle area and we had to clamp down. Consequently Les had to blow quite often which got the crowd on his back. The game suffered because of it but we were all refereeing to orders.

My first game in the middle was France against Fiji, again. This was to be in Grenoble, a beautiful part of France. We were all given a game in the middle, one on the side and one number four in the pools. Yagi, however, didn't get to referee! There was a rumour that because the Fijians had such an exciting back division the French were going to narrow the width of the pitch. But when I went to check the pitch before hand everything was fine, it was just another rumour in the press to add to the build up. Fiji just didn't perform and I was very disappointed. There was a distinct lack of spirit in their team. Even when I went to check their studs they were very quiet. Whether or not this was the way they prepared, I don't know. The French on the other hand were very pumped up and banging their chests and so forth. France played well, with Serge Blanco his usual mercurial self, and they won 33-9. France were determined to win all three of their pool matches. This certainly wasn't a classic, you have to have two teams who are willing to play for that.

Then it was on to Toulouse where I was number four in the Canada-Romania game with Sandy Macneil in the middle. The touch judges were Kerry Fitzgerald and Les. Canada were looking to grab second position and although it was a dull affair, a lot rested on the outcome. Canada won and went through to play the All Blacks in the quarter final. It was difficult to assess how well I'd done because the France-Fiji game wasn't that difficult to handle and there weren't any problems regarding foul play. But you'd be both a fool and a liar to say that you weren't concerned with your assessment, the cut is never far from your mind. Every time you went out to dinner with other referees it inevitably cropped up in the conversation. We wouldn't stab each other in the back so we tried to be complimentary about each other's performances. It's much easier to look good in a good game. You can work your socks off in a boring, dour game but receive no accolades. So there is an element of luck involved. Only some referees were given second games, because there weren't enough matches in the pool stages for everyone to have two games each. I ran touch for Les in his second game between England and the United States in Twickenham. Then, immediately afterwards I was asked to go to Leicester for the New Zealand-Italy match to be number one for Kerry, because Sandy Macneil was having knee problems. I had planned to be in Cardiff to see Wales play Western Samoa but I ended up listening to it on the radio instead. There was some controversy in this one when it was felt that Robert Jones had got back to minor the ball but a try was given to Western Samoa by the French referee, Patrick Robin.

At this time, I didn't know that referees were already being pencilled in for the quarter finals. Wales, of course, didn't qualify and the unexpected line-up meant a change in referees. There were mixed feelings for me because now, I was going to Murrayfield to referee Scotland against Western Samoa but Wales were no longer in the tournament. It's sad that what has been bad news for Wales has been good news for me. I've had opportunities in these tournaments because Wales haven't been successful, since 1987. At the quarter final stage, there would always be three other matches for me to be considered for and in a semifinal, another one. I felt though in 1991 that we didn't have the team to get to the final.

Scotland against Western Samoa was a magnificent occasion. I had two Australians running touch, Sandy and Kerry. As I'd only had pool matches in 1987, this was to be my first in the knockout stages. Murrayfield was full and Princess Anne was there to cheer on Scotland. The Hastings brothers and John Rutherford were part of a very talented Scottish side captained by the hooker Colin 'Very, Very' Deans. His nickname came from his habit in after-match speeches of complimenting the opposition by saying said it had been a "very, very hard game and you made it very, very difficult for us and we were very, very surprised to win". It was an amazing game. Samoa kicked off, Scotland caught the ball and Gavin Hastings ran smack into the Samoan forwards. This was to be their game plan, to take on Samoa up front. It was very demanding to referee. There were huge hits going in and it was physical, confrontational but good, honest, hard rugby with flair as well. It was a pleasure to be out in the middle with the teams. There was no nonsense, decisions were accepted and it was a game where a referee could impress. When I played advantage each side took it. Scotland won but Western Samoa made them fight all the way. They lost 28-6 but at the end of the game, they made a lap of honour and received a standing ovation from the crowd. I knew from the assessor afterwards that I received a good report and that night I was going to enjoy myself. The reception was to be at Watsonians, home club of the Hastings brothers. The Samoans hadn't had a drink of alcohol all through the tournament: they had concentrated fully on their rugby. They had really wanted to do well and although they were disappointed they felt they had made their mark: they had progressed further in the tournament than had been anticipated. I'd refereed my first quarter final and I hoped I'd made my mark, too. Theoretically these were two of the best eight teams in the world.

What a night it was! The camaraderie was magnificent, so were the speeches and the fun involved. The banter between the two sides was hilarious. We had watched France play England on television after the game and the Scots knew their opponents in the semifinal would be the English in Murrayfield, so they really let themselves go knowing they had a week before that momentous game. Out of all the after-match functions I have attended, this stands out by far. The speeches were comical and the Western Samoans wore the kilts. There were gifts from each side to the other – everything was in the true spirit of the game. The manager of the Western Samoan team was drinking what he called 'orgasms' and in his speech he said that he hadn't had so many 'orgasms' in all his life. They had enjoyed themselves so much that they requested to stay on for a few more days, but their pleas weren't heard by the tournament organisers.

After the quarter finals there were only four remaining matches to be selected for. I knew things had gone well. We were assessed on ten different aspects with an overall total. If you were weak in one aspect you could make up in other ways. But you had to have a fairly high mark in each area to be in contention. I was to survive the cut and because Wales were out I could be considered for any match. But Jim Fleming, for example, could only be considered for one of the semifinals – so his odds were long. David Bishop had had a torrid time in Paris in England's 19-10 victory over France. He did an outstanding job but, by God, he had to work hard. The other quarter had been refereed by Fred Howard in Lille, which saw a 29-13 New Zealand win over Canada. There were still other referees who hadn't involved at this stage, such as Steve Hilditch of Ireland and Kerry Fitzgerald of Australia, so the next round of appointments was eagerly anticipated.

The assessors were to meet on the Monday, or the Tuesday if there were travel problems. Videos were available so that all the assessors could see every referees' performance. The semifinals were Scotland against England in Murrayfield and Australia against New Zealand in Dublin. By now the first cut had been made. The referees from the emerging nations were going home and I bid farewell to Yagi-San. But two of the fourteen officials from the International Board countries would also have to be dropped. Peter Brooke said it had been a difficult choice and he just named the twelve who would remain. One advantage to a surname like Bevan is that whenever anything is announced in alphabetical order I get to know quickly if I'm in or not. If the first surname announced begins with a 'C' or a 'D' I know I'm knackered! Fortunately my name was came up and then the others were raced through. I was more than glad to hear my name, then I had to think which two hadn't been announced. I looked across at Les and I could see by his disappointed expression that he hadn't been included. When I saw that, my joy was tinged with a great deal of sadness for Les. As a social animal and as a supportive official there was none better in

Wales. He is an outstanding individual. He'd refereed two games and I'd run touch for him in both and couldn't understand the decision to omit him from the final stages.

The other referee to miss out was the Frenchman, Patrick Robin. Naturally, he was also disappointed but his omission led to controversy at the farewell dinner that evening. There was annoyance in the French camp because they felt that some of the referees kept on weren't fully fit. This was, of course, denied. René Hourquet, the French referee who had been kept on, was supportive of his fellow countryman. It was the first time that we'd experienced this sort of thing and it placed Owen Doyle of Ireland, who acted as interpreter between the French and the rest of us in a very difficult position. Hourquet arrived at the farewell dinner with his arm in a sling with bandages and plasters on his head and informed the committee that he was fully fit to be selected. This was a joke which turned sour for the French. By midnight, the arguments were still raging and Hourquet decided not to continue in the competition because Patrick Robin hadn't been included. We'd been a pretty happy family of referees, so it was a bad way to end things. As a result, Les was reinstated and that's how the competition continued. Those who were left picked themselves up and got on with the job. We felt that there must be a better method to reducing the number of officials.

Kerry Fitzgerald was given Scotland against England. I had tipped this and had been willing to bet on him. It was a battle of a game – just a stepping stone to the final. Jim Fleming got Australia against New Zealand in the other semifinal. We felt as referees that if someone was to do a semifinal he would be unlikely to get one of the two remaining matches – the final and third place play-off. Out of the four officials not involved at this stage, three of us didn't live far from Cardiff so we decided to go home for a few days. I invited Sandy Macneil to stay with me in Clydach and he was introduced to the Vardre club. They made a great fuss of him and we watched both semifinals on television there over the weekend. We reported back to Cardiff on the Sunday night for the weekend feedback. I think that Ken Rowlands, of the WRU, was more hopeful than I was about the being awarded the final. He wanted me to have it more than I wanted it! He had been superb throughout the tournament. Nothing was announced on the Monday. On the Tuesday, I went for a jog with Kerry around the grounds behind Cardiff Castle where the referees did most of their training. On the way back, we bumped into Barry Michael who was a District Representative with the WRU and the Tournament Liaison Officer for Scotland, who were staying in the Angel Hotel nearby. The Scots were in Cardiff to play against New Zealand in the third place play-off. We had a chat about things and Kerry and I wandered back to our hotel. Kerry was talking about his future, and wasn't sure how long he would continue refereeing. He was in his forties and had met a nice girl in Brisbane and was thinking about settling down. He was a fabulous chap.

When we arrived back at our hotel, Ken Rowlands was there to greet us. His face was a picture but he wasn't allowed to say anything. It had to come from Peter Brooke, who then came up to us and told me that I'd been selected to referee the World Cup Final in Twickenham. Kerry grabbed hold of me, he knew exactly how I felt and said, "At last, Bev, there are two of us. I'm fed up of being called 'The World Cup Final Referee'. Now there will be two of us!" I'll never forget his words. (Eight weeks later there would be only one of us. Kerry suffered a massive heart attack at his desk in the bank where he worked.)

Here I was, a Vardre boy, going to do a World Cup Final. It seemed just like a couple of years ago that I was refereeing New Dock Stars and Hendy and teams like that, and thinking the world of it. I couldn't believe it. Ken put his arms around me to congratulate me and then had to turn away because he was so emotional. It was also a great honour for Ken because it was his job to bring referees forward in Wales. And Les was selected as number four with David Bishop and Keith Lawrence of New Zealand as touch judges. Les's involvement also vindicated the WRU's selection process – its two referees were now to be officials in the Final. I went back to my room looked at myself in the mirror and said "Yes!" in a very loud voice. Then the media got to know and Radio Wales wanted an interview and the newspapers wanted photo-graphs. At first I revelled in the attention but I soon realised I had little time to myself. I had to ask the hotel receptionist to block all my calls, then got in touch with my mother, my brothers and my sister and, of course, my children. I received telegrams from all over the world, from people I'd never met. I had one from the former cricketer,

Colin Cowdrey. But the first one came from the Vardre. It said: "Make sure those English bastards don't win it".

Steve Hilditch from Ireland had been selected to referee the New Zealand vs Scotland third place play-off on the Wednesday night. It's a game that nobody really wants to play in and it wasn't a great spectacle, but he handled it very well. Then it was up to London on the Thursday. I didn't know how to prepare for the final because it was something totally new to me. Once I got to London the attention started again. Media interviews, messages of good luck, other referees wanting to wish me well. I was still on cloud nine. Everywhere I went, everyone wanted to talk about the game. The night before, the officials went out to dinner for a quiet meal. After a chat about the game I went to bed, but I couldn't sleep. I tossed and turned all night and made frequent trips to the bathroom. Fair play to the chambermaid, she'd put some extra toilet rolls there for me just in case. I was probably the first up for breakfast but I just picked at my food. We'd been warned about the traffic so we went out to Twickenham on the coach with the administrative officials. Everyone else was going to the pre-final reception, but as the match officials we just went for a walk around the ground.

Security was massive because the Queen and other members of the Royal Family were attending along with the Prime Minister. The Royal Box was just above the referee's dressing room, so the 'safe area' was going to be our changing room in the event of a problem. There was a little groundsman there who was getting very irate because he couldn't do his job properly – so he popped in to my dressing room for a chat. "It's murder out there, Mr Bevan," he said, "there are security guards everywhere, but probably the only person anyone will want to shoot afterwards is you!" Ken came in and he broke down in tears. I cried with him as well, it was quite emotional. We waited in the dressing rooms for a long time, then it was stud-checking time and both coaches wanted a chat about things. They wanted to point out what they perceived were illegal actions by the opposing team in previous matches. I listened to them politely but this is all part of pre-match hype and it had no effect on me whatsoever and I quickly got back to my own thoughts. The players were great, but they must have been at least as nervous as I was. It was the first time that any of us had been involved in a World Cup Final.

The red carpet was rolled out and we went to meet the Royal Family. The Queen came out along with Princess Anne, who is without doubt my favourite member of the Royal family. She's so down to earth. I'd met her before when I'd refereed Scotland. I'd also met her son, Peter. He had been wearing pin badges from Ireland, Scotland and England. So I told him I'd send him a Welsh pin badge, which I did. I received a lovely letter of thanks from him, and this was just for a 25p badge! He'd gone out of his way to do that. When Princess Anne came up to me in Twickenham she said, "Thank you for sending that badge. Did you get a thank you?" "Yes I did," I replied. "You'd better have," she said. It was incredible, here was the richest family in the world thanking me for sending a simple badge. We'd been told what the protocol for meeting the Royals was and that we were only to speak to them if we were spoken to. The Queen came along and said, "So you're in charge". I said, "I like to think that I am, ma'am".

Then the dignitaries went back to their seats and the match could start. All the players had been wound up in the changing rooms and I thought that I would have a job on my hands to cool things down on the pitch. But by the time all the introductions had been made, the players had calmed down. Just before I was about to blow the whistle, I thought of my dad. If only he were alive now to see me. I had a tear in my eye when I thought of how he had laughed when I told him that I was going to referee, because I'd been sent off myself. So not only was blowing that whistle to start the game a very proud moment for me, it was also a sad one that he wasn't alive to see it.

I blew and the World Cup Final started. It wasn't a classic. My dream had been that it would be a final that everyone would remember for years to come, but it wasn't. It was a really hard fought match where there was never more than a few points between the two sides. There was only one try, by the Australian prop Tony Daly, which was a scrappy affair. It came from a lineout, which developed into a maul and they rolled over from that. So it wasn't even spectacular. I was on the spot, so there could be no controversy. There was just one controversial incident in the match, when England were attacking mid-way through the second half. The ball went along the three-quarter line and David Campese cleverly went for a smother tackle and deliberately knocked the ball on, for which I awarded a penalty. The crowd screamed for a penalty try. There was no doubt in my mind that it was a penalty as had I glanced behind me to see that there was cover coming across. So I felt that I couldn't give a penalty try because the cover would have got there.

The game ended 12-6 to Australia, and went by so quickly I couldn't believe it. From the moment I blew the final whistle it was Australia's day. I stayed on the pitch with the other officials for the presentations. England went up first to receive their runners-up medals. I followed and was presented with a platinum medal. The other officials went up after me and we all applauded when Australia lifted the trophy.

It had gone reasonably well for me. Then it was back to the dressing room for a chat and a nice hot bath. All the tension of the build up and the game and the lack of sleep the previous night caught up with me. I was mentally and physically exhausted. I just wanted to go to bed. I was so tired that I couldn't even really enjoy the post-match functions.

I thought that my decision not to award a penalty try would probably be a talking point, and I wasn't wrong. One or two of the media questioned me about it afterwards. They were looking for reasons why England had lost the game, but Jon Webb, the England full back, was quick to offer me support – I have a great deal of respect for the man. The TV replays vindicated my decision and Stephen Jones printed a diagram of the incident in *The Sunday Times* and he agreed with me, too. There was a general feeling that, in the final, England hadn't played their normal game, which had be so successful in the quarters and semis. The England players Peter Winterbottom and Mike Teague told me that they had given Australia too much respect.

I travelled home on the Sunday and, on the Monday I phoned Ken and asked him if I could have the following Saturday off. We were still in the middle of our domestic season, so there was a full league programme. Ken agreed but then rang me back on the Thursday and asked me to be a touch judge in the match between Bridgend and Newport. I reluctantly agreed – but I couldn't refuse Ken. As I ran across to the scoreboard side at the Brewery Field, the announcer congratulated me on the final and the crowd applauded, which I thought was nice of them. At the second line out, the referee penalised Newport and someone in the crowd behind me shouted "Well done ref, Bevan wouldn't have seen that!" So it was World Cup Final one week and then back down to earth with a bump the next – fabulous!

The World Cup Years – 1995

The 1995 World Cup in South Africa was held out of season for us. This time the two Welsh referees were Clayton Thomas and myself, and since South Africa was to be involved for the first time there would be extra referees from their country. The format was similar to 1987 and 1991 and the appointments were to be made for the pool matches by the RWC Referees Appointments Committee headed by Tom Doocey of New Zealand. My old refereeing tutor, Gwyn Watts was again the assessor from Wales. I had refereed Scotland against France in the preceding Five Nations and New Zealand against France when France won its first series in New Zealand. I had had a good season in the run up, so I was feeling pretty positive.

The referees arrived in Johannesburg a week before the tournament began, to acclimatize to the altitude. We were given a talk by the Chief of Police and warned about the dangers of the city and that crime was such a big problem there. We were told not to hire any cars but to rely on the appointed drivers to be driven around. We were told about the muggings and the murders. We should not wear any jewellery. If somebody shoved a gun or a knife into our face we should give them what they wanted and then we might survive. If somebody was being mugged on the other side of the street we were not to cross and help – we should try to stay out of it. Where possible we had to stay in twos or threes. We were staying in a good part of the city and everything we wanted was to be found there: the restaurants, bars and shops. Some journalists would later be mugged and two of the All Blacks attacked outside their hotel. We were to be very alert. The hotel management would tell us where to go and where not to go. There was security everywhere – at the main doors and outside the lifts.

I knew when I arrived in South Africa that I wouldn't be in contention for the final. It was only the third World Cup and no-one was going to do two finals. It was indicated to me 'unofficially' through conversations with the Appointments Panel, when it came up in conversation that I already had done a final. Although no one said anything outright there were certainly hints. But the appointments panel gave me everything but the final. I was appointed for the opening match between the hosts and the holders – South Africa against Australia – a huge game. I felt more pressure in this one than in any other match. It was the opening game of the World Cup – in South Africa – it was their first time in the World Cup and they were hosting the tournament. The match was in Cape Town and the city was alive. There were new laws to enforce, particularly at the line out. The referees had been working hard all week on this aspect and both sets of team management wanted clarification and confirmation. The new law was that once a player was in the air, then support was allowed – but he had to get up there on his own. All eyes would be on me to see how I would interpret this and other new laws.

There was also the opening ceremony to contend with. I thought that Wales and New Zealand were rugby mad but in South Africa interest was on another level. The country was so expectant and I could only imagine what the pressure on the Springboks was like. When we arrived in Cape Town every bar, shop window were decorated in green and gold: it was a massive rugby city. Our hotel was a stone's throw from the ground so there was no escaping it.

My touch judges were Clayton and Steve Hilditch of Ireland. We were down in the dressing rooms long before kick off but we had to be because of the opening ceremony. There was so much happening it was easy to forget that there was actually a game of rugby to be played. I only saw bits of the ceremony through the tunnel but I couldn't take it in anyway. I was trying hard to focus on the game and not be distracted. I hadn't been told how to referee the game. We were told that the Panel would be supportive of us but didn't want the referees to be the focus of attention. I had been given an old whistle which had been used to start the previous World Cups. It was normally housed in a museum in Wellington, and had belonged to a famous New Zealand referee. Nelson Mandela was there and he came to see us before the game. He asked me "How is my friend Maggie Thatcher?" He had an aura about him. It was the first of three occasions we met him. The second was at a function for referees at his palace in Pretoria and then again in the Final. The match itself went very well, it was a cracking game of rugby and worthy of the opening match in the World Cup. There were no major incidents. It was hard and physical but a perfect start for me and both teams were complimentary.

For the first time also, one of the emerging nations' referees was to be given a game. He was a Korean who spoke no English, and I was to run touch for him. A Canadian referee was on the other touch and Steve Lander of England was the number four. The fixture was France against the Ivory Coast, which will be remembered for the sad incident in which one of the Ivory Coast players was paralysed. (When players are stretchered off the field you really don't know how badly injured they are. It was forty-eight hours later before we knew the full extent of the injury.) We realized there would be a language problem and, pre-match, we had an interpreter with us so the referee could give us our orders. But I thought that even if I flagged for foul play how would I tell him what I'd seen? The interpreter couldn't come from the stand each time for me to explain to him for him to then explain to the referee. It would be a farce.

As the game developed France wanted to play some good rugby and the Ivory Coast wanted to stop them. This frustrated the French. There was ball-killing and jersey-pulling but it was difficult for me to help the referee. I shouted at some of the players about offside. There was a line out at which the ball went back on the French side and as the ball went out to the outside half, the French prop pulled an Ivory Coast player back by his jersey. The Ivory Coast player turned, punched him and ran away. I flagged and the Frenchman smiled because he knew I'd seen the incident. But I wondered how the hell I was going to explain all of this to the Korean referee. Then I thought – to hell with it and put my flag down! All the games were televised so I thought that this would be picked up. But I'd made my decision and France were the easy winners by 54-18. Overall, the Korean referee did an excellent job and had done his country proud. At the post-match function the French prop came up to me and asked me why I had put my flag down. I told him "Number one, you pulled him back. Number two, he punched you. Number three, you got what you deserved. Number four, the referee speaks no English and had a good game, so everyone's happy." He started laughing and held his jaw and said "Well maybe not everybody." When I saw a replay of the game, the cameras had followed the ball so it hadn't been spotted. It was the only time that I ever did that, but to this day I still don't know how I would have explained it all to the referee.

The next game was South Africa against Canada, which was the first one to blow up. There were three sendings-off (James Dalton from South Africa, Rod Snow and Gareth Rees from Canada) and the incidents in this match, which South Africa won 20-0, would have a bearing on one of the semifinals. The referee was David McHugh of Ireland. He and I went for a drink to an Irish bar one evening shortly afterwards. Several South African supporters there got quite abusive towards David and the bar owner asked us to leave for our own safety. My other on-field involvement was to run touch for Clayton in the Italy-Argentina game. Clayton was a little disappointed because it was the last round of pool matches and both teams were already going home – they were only playing for pride. So after that big start the remainder of the pool games were quite quiet for me.

Off the field, we had plenty of opportunity to see the country. Despite its many problems, South Africa is a spectacular place. We couldn't visit without the obligatory trip to a game reserve. A group of referees went to the Kruger National, but we didn't see many animals. It's an enormous park, almost the size of Wales. So you could be in Swansea and the elephants could be in Pembrokeshire! Our guide with us desperately tried to find some animals for us to see. We'd come across a tree knocked down and he'd say "Elephants!" But there were none to be seen. The we'd come across piles of dung and he'd say "Rhinoceros!" But again there were none about. It was a hard day's travelling and we did come across what was left of a kill, but that was about it.

The authorities in South Africa didn't hide anything from us. On another occasion we went into the township of Soweto, but in armoured cars with armed guards. We had peep holes to look out through. We also visited the grave of the first person to be killed in the troubles. The armed guards got out first to check that everything was clear before we were allowed to disembark ourselves. We saw that we were about a hundred yards away from a school. The Australian assessor was with us and he decided to hand some pin badges out to the children who had come to the fence. They flocked around him and when the children were sent away by the security guards, he realized he'd lost his wallet, his credit cards and all his money! They'd picked him dry. We visited Soweto Hospital. There is so much violence in Soweto surgeons from all over the world visit there for training, particularly on the treatment of gunshot wounds. We also met a nightclub owner with a huge Cadillac. He smoked a big cigar and was surrounded by bodyguards. I asked him whether anybody had tried to steal his car. He told me "Nobody would dare, they know who it belongs to!" I understood why.

The pool matches were completed and again Wales hadn't qualified. In these tournaments, as a referee, I didn't get much chance to mix with the Welsh team. Referees are always in a different pool to their own country and based elsewhere. I saw Wales against Ireland in East London airport on the way back to Johannesburg from being touch judge for Clayton in the Italy-Argentina match – we were two very depressed Welshmen. It's good to be able to chat with the Welsh boys when you can, it's something you can't really do with the other teams. You have to let them come to talk to you in after-match functions, particularly the coaches. I've seen some referees go up to coaches and ask them what they thought of their refereeing performance. What an invitation to give a coach! I've usually tried to stay in the background, but I am always delighted to speak to a coach or a captain afterwards if they are seeking clarification about something. If you penalise a side ten times in a lineout then I believe that a coach is entitled to ask you why. You could be saving him ten penalties in the next game. In South Africa all the after-match functions were buffets and very often the teams were back on a plane to their base shortly afterwards, so there wasn't too much contact.

The dreaded cut came round. As expected, all the referees from the emerging countries were on the list, together with Barry Lees of Australia and Ken McCartney of Scotland. Ken was bitterly disappointed and angry. Barry was half expecting it but it wasn't pleasant for him. I really felt for Ken. We had developed a close friendship over the years and I was saddened he had been deselected. I hadn't seen the game which he'd refereed. A 'celebration' dinner was held to say goodbye to everyone. For the emerging countries it is a big occasion but for people like Barry and Ken it was a terrible way to finish. The function was in a Johannesburg city centre hotel and security meant that we were ushered everywhere by armed guards.

In the quarter finals I was given New Zealand against Scotland in Pretoria, about an hour from Johannesburg. On the way there we passed the Mint where they make the Krugerrands – and the trophies for the tournament finalists and the four officials. My quarter final touch judges were Wayne Ericsson of Australia and Clayton, and the number four was Joel Dumé of France. Gavin Hastings was the Scotland captain and Sean Fitzpatrick led the All Blacks. They'd had a good tournament and were really up for it. By now, the big man on the scene was Jonah Lomu. The pre-match atmosphere was superb, as you would expect for any game involving Scotland. Their supporters were there in their kilts and ginger wigs. And the All Blacks had phenomenal following, too.

New Zealand played some marvellous rugby, Lomu did a lot of damage and at one stage ran through both Hastings brothers. The All Blacks ran up an early lead and although Scotland came back to end at 48-30, it wasn't enough. It was a really good game of rugby without it being one-sided and Scotland came off the park with a great deal of credit. New Zealand were reasonably happy with their performance, and mine. There were no complaints from Scotland either. It was a straightforward game from my point of view. Although I realized the final would be out for me I was far from thinking that the tournament was over from my perspective. I love the big match atmosphere whether as a referee, touch judge or number four. I love to walk around before the kick off and look at the stadium and the crowd. It's wonderful to be part of it and to stand for the anthems, whether it's the long Italian one or the rousing French. I still get shivers down my spine when an anthem is sung before a game. You really feel like singing along with 'Flower of Scotland' but I'm sure the All Blacks might have something to say about that. Even when I'm sitting at home watching an international on the television I feel envious of the referee unless it's an awful game.

Jim Fleming had his work cut out in the South Africa against Western Samoa and there'd been some controversy regarding big hits. Ireland were beaten by France, and thanks to Rob Andrew's drop goal England went through against Australia. David Bishop from New Zealand was in the middle for this one and was tipped for the final. But like a lot of his countrymen before him, the success of the national side meant limited opportunities for New Zealand referees in the World Cup. After the quarters the assessors linked up with us on the Monday morning for feedback, then the appointments for the semis were made.

We knew by now that they would be South Africa against France the following Saturday and England against New Zealand on Sunday. I got the first along with my quarter final touch judges, Clayton and Wayne, with Jim as number four. It was another great honour for me because it meant I had refereed at every stage in a World Cup. Because my country wasn't involved I could be considered for any game, although the other referees had to wait for the results of matches before knowing if they could be involved or not. The other semifinal was to be refereed by my good friend Steve Hilditch, probably the finest personality in world refereeing, a head teacher from Belfast. He's wonderful narrator and whenever we referees needed someone to speak on our behalf, he was the one. I cannot praise him highly enough. He was also on his third World Cup and decided to retire after the semifinal – and what a game to end on.

During the week before our semi everyone was talking about the state of the pitch. Durban is a seaside town and a real surfers' paradise. When you opened the curtains of the hotel bedroom the view was fantastic, a real beautiful setting. The evening before the match the officials were invited to the home of the President of the Durban Referees. He lived in a magnificent house in the mountains above the town. We had a lovely evening and we were told that the weather forecast for the following day wasn't too good, but our hosts assured us with a "Don't worry, it never rains in Durban". Although we only had a couple of glasses of wine I didn't sleep at all well.

The following morning, the heavens opened. A huge black cloud moved overhead and it was as if day had turned into night. All along the sea-front in Durban, traders sell their wares on the side of the pavement. When the rain came down they scattered everywhere and rushed to scoop up their belongings. There was terrific thunder and lightening. A few of us had been having a stroll and we were soaked through by the time we made it back to the hotel. It was hammering down. As the morning passed the rain didn't relent.

It was still raining when we got out to the ground and somebody suggested that I had better take a look at the pitch. The groundsman was sitting in his office with his feet up on the desk, smoking a cigarette. I asked him for a pair of wellington boots so that I could inspect the pitch. He didn't have any. He told me they weren't needed because "It never rains in Durban". I told him it certainly was raining if he hadn't noticed and I asked him what their plans were. They had no plans. I keep my boots in plastic bags. On that day they happened to be in Tesco bags so I put these over my shoes and strapped them to my trousers so I could inspect the pitch. It was about 90 minutes before the kick off and my shoes were disappearing under the water. I realized that there was no way the game could proceed under these conditions. If a maul or a ruck collapsed, or there would be a pile-up, players faced a real danger of drowning. Safety is of paramount importance so I wasn't going to let anything like that happen.

I went back into the dressing room and told Clayton and Wayne that I wasn't prepared to start the game. It was still raining heavily so things were getting worse. I went back to see the groundsman who was still sitting in his office, and still had no plans. By now the IRB officials were beginning to arrive along with the teams. The captains and coaches came to see me and I told them that I wasn't prepared to start the game, and complained that nothing was being done about the situation. I had suggested a pump to clear the water, but nothing had happened.

The stadium was beginning to fill with supporters and slowly, the clock was ticking away. Terry Vaux and Brian Jones from Wales were there for the game and they popped in to say hello. I was glad to see some familiar faces from back home, as I was about to stop a World Cup semifinal from starting. Then Louis Luyt, the President of the South African Rugby Union arrived along with Marcel Martin of France who was the Match Commissioner with the IRB. They wanted to know what was happening and the truth was that nothing was happening. It was getting wetter and wetter and the water on the pitch was getting deeper and deeper. We were getting closer to kick off time. At one stage we counted twenty-two people in the referees' room – and it's not a big one.

At last we had some constructive suggestions to solve the problem. The first thing mentioned was postponing the game until the following day, but that was ruled out of the question because flights were booked and hotel rooms were fixed up – there were practical reasons why postponement wasn't an option. Then someone asked what would happen if the game was abandoned permanently. Who would go through? Would it be on the toss of a coin? Everyone went diving into the rules of the competition. It was found that the result would be decided on discipline, and because South Africa had a man sent off in the game against Canada it looked as if France would then go through. Louis Luyt went white when he heard this. I was standing next to him and I could hear him speaking to the groundsman on his mobile, and he said "I don't give a ****, get that water off the pitch now – even if you've got to drink it! Don't worry, you won't have a job by this time tomorrow if that water isn't cleared!" I then declared that the kick off would be put back by thirty minutes.

Pumps were now sent for. The whisper had got around that France might go through if the match wasn't played. I did many television and radio interviews and was under a tremendous amount of pressure even though the game hadn't started. Everywhere I went someone was sticking a microphone or camera in my face. I went up in the lift to where all the IRB dignitaries were. There the talk was of bringing in a helicopter to get rid of the water. But then we saw the women come on to the pitch with their brushes and mops to physically sweep the water away. Everyone in the room looked very embarrassed by this.

It was obvious we wouldn't get a three-thirty kick off so we put it back again to four-fifteen. Again there were more interviews to be given but the rain had stopped. We phoned the airport for a weather forecast and they assured us that we had seen the last of the rain.

That was some good news at last. The crowd was getting agitated by now because of the hour and a quarter delay, but no-one left the ground. Both teams were magnificent about it and very supportive. Everyone understood the situation. If this had been a league match back in Wales it wouldn't have been played. But these were totally different circumstances: a full stadium of sixty thousand people with another semifinal the following day, every opportunity had to be given for the game to proceed. Safety of the players must come first but the pressure was immense.

The good thing was that everyone involved wanted the game to go on, so at least there was a positive attitude. The water level went down, we checked the pitch and I was happy that the game could now proceed. I had prepared myself to referee a classic but now conditions would be different, it would be a war of attrition. I told the players beforehand that there would be a lot of mistakes and the ball would be like a bar of soap. At least the conditions were the same for both sides. I said that I would try to let the game go but if a side couldn't take an advantage then I would have to blow up. This would mean a lot of scrums and I wouldn't stand for any messing about there. I would come down hard on them. In fairness to the six front row players they did very well, common sense prevailed and they didn't mess me around.

Despite the weather forecast, it rained again ten minutes into the game. South Africa scored the first try but there wasn't much between them. The game built up and towards the end France were pounding the South African line looking for the winning score. The French forwards drove on towards the try-line but Benazzi was brought down inches short and lost the ball allowing South Africa to clear their lines. Some viewed this as a controversial incident and my decision not to award a try was questioned. But there was no doubt in my mind that he hadn't scored. My positioning was good and the touch judge also supported. I've looked at it many times since then on video and I am still happy. The big plus though was Benazzi himself. When he was interviewed after the game he said he was so close to putting France into the final. I could have hugged him. He could have said something which wasn't true and the whole of France would have believed him. A camera showed he was inches short of the line. The camera had proved me wrong in the game between Australia and New Zealand in 1986, but this time it was on my side. I don't think I've been so physically and mentally drained as I was at the end of this semifinal. The French were marvellous in defeat and it was the first time that I had refereed them when they lost. I saw Louis Luyt after the game and told him "if anyone else tells me that it never rains in Durban – I'll hit them."

The other semifinal was played the following day and we had the final that everyone wanted, South Africa against New Zealand. We had our usual debriefing sessions on the Monday and contemplated the remaining appointments. David Bishop couldn't now be considered for the final. But he got the third place play-off, which came as no surprise and that would be his last international. It was a shame that one of the finest referees in world rugby never got to officiate at a World Cup final because of the success of his national side. It was announced that Ed Morrison of England would referee the final. I was his number one touch judge, Joel Dumé of France was on the other touch, with Clayton as number four. So for the second successive World Cup Final, there were two Welsh officials involved. On a personal basis, I had now officiated in every role in the final, number four in 1987, referee in 1991, and now touch judge in 1995.

I was delighted and thrilled for Ed Morrison. Ed was different to your average English referee, a lot of whom I found to be rather full of themselves. Perhaps Ed was different because he lived close to the Welsh border! Bristol, Gloucester and Bath are certainly different to your Harlequins and Saracens. Ed is a down to earth guy and everyone was pleased for him. He'd had a good tournament, gone about his business in a no-nonsense fashion and kept his nose clean. The RFU were also thrilled and they flew Mrs Morrison out to join her husband. It was a wonderful gesture on their part and typical of them.

The third place play-off was held on the Thursday before the Final and we were all invited to watch England play France in Pretoria. It was a very poor match between two sides who didn't really want to be there even though there was the incentive that the side which finished in third place wouldn't have to qualify for the tournament in 1999. David Bishop deserved a far better game than this to finish his career. France won it 19-9 but there didn't seem to be many people who really cared.

All the focus was now on the Final in Johannesburg. My brother Wyn came out to join me and wanted to be a part of the big day. I gave him my pass as everyone at the stadium knew me by now. He met all the players and had a great day there. We officials got to the ground very early – even though there were no worries about the weather. Ed was quite relaxed and soon it was time to check the studs. I found the New Zealand dressing room to be unusually subdued. I had refereed them several times before and normally they would be buzzing. Later there were rumours that they were suffering from food poisoning. We didn't meet Mandela before the game this time.

There were no tries in the game itself which was nip and tuck. Every time there was a stoppage in the play, African music was played loudly to motivate the crowd and their team. Thanks to Joel Stransky's dropped goal their dream came true. Skydivers came down with banners wishing everyone farewell and good luck to Wales in 1999. The host nation had reached the final in every World Cup so far: Wales would have to improve to keep the record going.

We all thought that the after-match function would be special because the hosts had won, but I didn't realise that I would remember it for the wrong reasons. The officials had a few drinks together and it was an opportunity to exchange addresses and telephone numbers and to mull over the tournament in general. All the World Cup dignitaries were present along with the four teams involved in the last two matches. The setting in the hotel was fit for a king. There were big screens everywhere and the referees were allocated two tables. We were shown a video looking back at the tournament and of South Africa itself. It was quite biased towards South Africa's participation but, well, I suppose they won. There were speeches from the organizers and an exchange of gifts. Then Louis Luyt got up to speak and make some presentations. He started speaking about referees so we all pricked our ears up at this. He thought the tournament had gone well from this aspect, which isn't difficult to say when you've just won it. Then he called me up to receive a gift. I thought this was a bit strange because I was only a touch judge in the final so Ed should go up first. But I thought perhaps he was doing it alphabetically, so I went up to the stage. I had no choice because it would have been very awkward to have refused. But I didn't know what it was about anyway, so I had no reason to think that I shouldn't go up.

Luyt thanked me and presented a gift. I thanked him, walked back to my seat and waited to see who would be next. I thought nothing more of it. The presentation was a small box, about four inches square and gift wrapped, so I couldn't see what it was. Then he went on to talk about something else and I started to feel very uncomfortable. Jim Fleming was sitting next to me and Steve Lander opposite. Jim asked me, "What is it?" I replied, "I don't know and I don't think I want to know." I had this feeling that people were watching me and when I turned around, the journalists were all looking over. This made me more uncomfortable. Jim grabbed the box and opened it. On the lid it was inscribed 'Presented to W.D. Bevan, Referee'. Inside there it was – a pocket watch with the Rugby World Cup emblem and logo on it. People then started asking me why did I get it? I couldn't answer them because I didn't know. The officials had already been presented with the Krugerrand trophies. A lot of people weren't happy that I'd been singled out for a gift, and I certainly wasn't happy about it myself. Louis Luyt went on a bit and the ill-feeling was spreading around the room. As the days went by, the 'value' of this damn watch went up from being worth £100 to £1,000. One South African newspaper said it was worth £3,000 and back home one report said it was worth £5,000. I didn't know what to do, whether or not to give it back.

The following morning, the Manager of the South African team, Morne Du Plessis, came to see me along with the Secretary of the South African Rugby Board, and apologized profusely. They said that the presentation hadn't been planned. Louis Luyt had done it off his own back and they were sorry for any embarrassment caused. The advice from the WRU was not to return the watch and that the whole incident would die a death. But it certainly didn't. Back home, within an hour of my return to work I must have been asked for the time about forty or fifty times. It went on for weeks and weeks. Every game I refereed, every penalty decision I made, there would be some comment. If I was close to the crowd people would shout, "What time is it Bevan?" If there was a debatable decision I would hear, "You'll get another watch for this!"

I spoke at a dinner at Neath Athletic whose President was Tony

Lewis, the cricketer. At the end they presented me with a plastic watch about four feet long. I was half-way through a speech at Ynysybwl Rugby Club – Ken Rowlands' club – when someone emerged from the toilet and shouted out "Has anyone lost a watch?" So while the watch was embarrassing at the time it's also been a tool of great humour over the past few years. In the early stages I got really fed up with it. But then I went along with it and would tap my wrist and smile whenever someone made a comment. Now I use it to my benefit at dinners. I did have the watch valued when I returned from the World Cup. The jeweller in Clydach had heard all about the watch and was delighted to put a value on it. I was told it was quite a basic piece worth about £90! At first I thought of donating it to charity but when I found it wasn't worth that much I didn't want to embarrass a charity because it wouldn't raise that much money for them. So I've still got it and it's collecting dust in my drawer.

The World Cup Years – 1999, Wales

There was a big change in the appointment of referees for the 1999 Rugby World Cup. The IRB had now assumed responsibility for all international refereeing appointments so the home unions were no longer able to nominate their own officials. Selection was to be merit-based, depending on form in tournaments leading up to the World Cup such as the European Cup, Super 12, Tri-Nations and the Five Nations. I had had a good year and it was a good time to have three internationals – Scotland vs Ireland, New Zealand vs Australia and Ireland vs Argentina. I went to Murrayfield expecting a battle royal between Scotland and Ireland. The Irish had disrupted other teams with their aggressive front row play but it was quite simply a great game of rugby won 24-15 by the Scots. It was the old story of two sides wanting to play rugby and what great entertainment they produced. It's lovely when you expect a dour game and two sides produce a top quality occasion.

It was Scotland's year and they pipped England to the Championship. Strangely, I saw every game involving Scotland live. I was on touch for England vs Scotland, in the crowd for Wales vs Scotland, I refereed Scotland vs Ireland and was on touch for France vs Scotland. For the Scotland vs Ireland game my microphone was, for the first time, linked to the IRB assessor, so he could hear what I was saying to the players. He was an English assessor and he gave me a good mark, the lovely chap. I didn't know until after the game that he could hear me but I like to think that I wouldn't have altered my style. Bill McClaren, the commentator could also hear what I was saying, but I could only hear my touch judges.

Then it was out to New Zealand for the Tri-Nations where I did three appointments – touch judge for New Zealand vs South Africa in Wellington, across to Brisbane to be on touch for Australia vs South Africa, then back to Auckland to referee New Zealand vs Australia. These were immense matches between three teams who would command semifinal places in the coming World Cup. The last match was the first Tri-Nations game to be played under floodlights and was, as usual, a complete sell-out. Eden Park in Auckland had been completely revamped. It was a top class game of rugby with two sides playing at their best and I tried to be unobtrusive as New Zealand won 34-15. Floodlights can be quite an advantage for the referee, better than a sunny day where a low sun can affect your vision. I don't think the players themselves are so keen because it's a long day waiting for the kick off. But it's a tremendous spectacle for the fans.

I had decided to go for selection for the 1999 World Cup and was trying to produce my best performances. You need a bit of luck in your matches: both sides must want to play rugby. If you can't referee that sort of game then you'll never succeed. I had another English assessor for the Auckland test: Colin High an ex-international referee himself, and once again he was complimentary. He told me that I wouldn't be a role model for refereeing but my experience carried me through. He also said that at times I was taking short cuts, maybe spending more time at the back of the line out than I should. I countered by pointing out where the ball was being thrown and that I had refereed these teams often enough to know their lineout signals. If George Gregan, the Australian scrum half, rubbed one finger on his nose then I knew it was going to the back of the lineout. Colin High was correct, of course. I was spending a lot more time at the back of the lineout to be closer to the action.

I knew I had one more international to impress, Ireland vs Argentina in Dublin, my favourite venue. I hoped that another good performance would clinch my RWC selection. I would say that, in Wales, four of us had our fingers crossed: myself, Clayton, Robert Davies and Nigel Whitehouse. A week before this international Argentina had beaten Scotland in Murrayfield, a sign, perhaps, of the coaching of Alex 'Grizz' Wylie, the former All Black back row player. It was another good game of rugby and the assessment, by a

Frenchman, went well. Ireland won 32-24 although Argentina staged a comeback towards the end.

In all, I was fairly relaxed about my selection because the season's internationals had gone so well, with no controversy at all. The IRB for the first time were going to appoint referees and touch judges who would just run the line. The referees would be there for the whole tournament. The IRB selection committee would chose fourteen referees and twelve touch judges, who knew they would be redundant after the pool matches. The referees would then carry on for the remainder of the tournament and run touch. This formula got rid of the ludicrous deselection process of the previous tournaments which had produced so much bad feeling. The list was published and comprised five officials from Australia, five from New Zealand, three from South Africa. In Wales we only had two: Clayton and myself, the same as in 1995.

The IRB put forward the criteria for referees fitness, which we all had to pass. It involved the dreaded bleep test and a three thousand metre run – seven and a half laps of the track. You had to pass these fitness tests with your own Union and then again a week before the World Cup tournament itself started. We were told that anyone failing this test would be sent home. This seemed rather self-defeating because the IRB were flying officials to Wales from all over the world and they might have to send some of them back again straight away.

I had passed my domestic fitness test and I had no trouble with the bleep test. The referees and touch judges congregated in Cardiff and were well kitted-out. We were also given shirts, ties, blazers, trousers and wet weather gear. Steve Griffiths, the IRB Referees Development Officer had done a marvellous job for us. But – crunch time – we now had to pass the World Cup fitness test. All the officials jumped on the bus which took us to the University of Wales Institute in Cardiff for the tests. It was a very nervous bus indeed. Although people were fit there was still the threat of being sent home if you failed, and it wouldn't have been far for me, only forty miles down the M4. I'd seen some of the other officials in action and this was going to be a doddle for them. Some were in their thirties, professional referees for whom the fitness test would be like a stroll in the park. I was fifty-two and had only been doing a couple of stints in the gym every week on the way home from work. Clayton, who is a P.E. teacher is extremely fit, but even he was a bit nervous. I thought that I might struggle along with Jim Fleming, Joel Dumé and Didier Mené, who didn't quite look like athletes.

We were given the option of either doing the bleep tests or the three thousand metre run because the IRB people wanted the tests over in the morning session. As a result you couldn't do both – not that I wanted to anyway! As long as you passed one or the other you were through. There was a lot of banter on the bus and questions flying around about who was going to do which test. I had done the three thousand metre run before, but on a running machine not on a track. You can set the machine and off you go, but running around a track is completely different so I opted for the bleep test. It was decided that the three thousand metres would be completed first. So the likes of Paddy O'Brien and Colin Hawke of New Zealand and other very fit referees started the run. They had done it many times before and they knew exactly what they had to do: three thousand metres in twelve and a half minutes. They had their lap targets written on their hands and they were keeping time with their own stop watches – very professional indeed. It was a stroll for them, they weren't even sweating or breathing heavily. The rest of us were watching this and we thought it looked easy. Fleming thought it looked easier than the bleep test. At the end of the run six of them crossed the line together, holding their hands in the air with about twenty seconds to spare. They could have done it again without any bother at all.

Then some of us made a dreadful mistake. Jim Fleming, Ed Morrison, Brian Campsall, Steve Lander, Clayton and myself decided to opt for the run instead of the bleep test. It very nearly proved to be my downfall. Campsall would be the pace setter and we'd all tuck in behind him. After a lap, I was heaving. The only consolation was that Fleming, alongside me, was in greater difficulty. He realized he wasn't going to make it and dropped out after the first lap. I thought it would look bad if I did the same so I tried to stick with the rest of them. The second lap was worse, the third was hard, the fourth was tough. I was only half way and knew I was struggling. I had to go on now because there was no way I would have enough energy to go through the bleep test after this. Suddenly a gap was opening up between Campsall, Morrison, Clayton and Lander and myself. Lander is a full time professional referee who could do the bleep test in his sleep but he'd fallen into the trap.

We were now regretting our foolish decision. On the fifth lap, it was quite noticeable that I was having problems. I was dropping back further. Some of the others who had completed the run started to encourage me from the sidelines. Paddy O'Brien ran alongside me shouting encouragement. I felt like giving up but he kept me going. I was on the last lap, then on the home straight and I picked up my speed a little and came home eight seconds to spare. I just collapsed on the floor. Without a doubt had it not been for Paddy's encouragement I would never have done it and I would have been going home. The bleep test started only five minutes later so there would have been no way I could have recovered. I was absolutely knackered.

We were all very relieved and went to watch Fleming in the bleep test. He was always in front of the bleep and passed. I don't think the IRB wanted to fail anyone but I very nearly put them to the test and my tournament would have been over before a whistle had been blown. And I wouldn't have had the breath to blow it! The atmosphere on the bus on the way back to the hotel was completely different and I had my leg pulled as the 'old man' of the tournament.

Another new law regarding supporting in the lineout had been introduced just a week before the tournament and the coaches were very unhappy about it. Anyone supporting in the line out had to have his hands on the jumper's shorts not on his skin. This was to prevent the jumper being lifted dangerously high. Common sense from the referee can sort this out, but it was another thing for us to contemplate after the rigours of the fitness test.

The appointments were announced for the pool matches. There were fourteen referees and twenty-six pool matches, so all the referees, except for two, would have two pool matches each. Colin Hawke and myself were the odd ones out, but we were given the two quarter final play-off games. Mine was to be in Murrayfield. We would all be assessed on our performances before the appointments for the quarter finals were made. The Referees Committee appointed teams of four officials, who would take charge of matches on Saturdays and Sundays. The number four official on the Saturday would then referee the game the following day and the referee from the Saturday would be the number four the following day. The two touches would be the same for both games. Paddy O'Brien was selected for the opening game between Wales and Argentina at the Millennium Stadium, and because I wasn't on duty until the following day I went along to enjoy the opening ceremony and the game. I thought the ceremony was fantastic and there was a great atmosphere in the stadium. There were complaints that it didn't reflect an international theme but it was OUR World Cup, so the more Welsh it was the better!

My first appointment was as number four on the first Saturday for England vs Italy in Twickenham and then I would be in the middle for New Zealand vs Tonga at Ashton Gate in Bristol on the Sunday. The other members of our team were Andre Watson and Tappa Henning of South Africa, and Ian Hyde-Lay, a touch judge from Canada. England looked very impressive in the game against Italy and played some good, open and attractive rugby. Thankfully we had no need of another new disciplinary initiative, the citing system. In the past, if the referee or touch judge had spotted foul play and had dealt with it either with a ticking off, a yellow or red card then, other than an appeal by the player, that was the end of the matter. But now there was be a neutral citing commissioner who, at the instigation of one of the teams, could look at video replays of any incident on the field of play in detail. It was used in the very first game after which Colin Charvis of Wales and Roberto Grau of Argentina were cited and received a ban.

It also happened to me in my first game in the middle, at Ashton Gate. There was a lot of hype surrounding the match between New Zealand and Tonga. Amazingly, this was the first time the two sides had met in a Test match. The All Blacks fielded a full strength side. The Tongan coach was from South Africa and he told me that they were really up for it and they were going to meet New Zealand head on! And he was true to his word. Tonga had a contingent of players who played in Wales and there was some Welsh support for them. Ironically, the first controversial incident involved the Ebbw Vale full back, Siua 'Josh' Taumalolo. The All Blacks caught the ball from the kick off and they were driven back ferociously at the first maul which set the scene for what was to come.

The game was only ninety seconds old when Jonah Lomu got the ball and Taumalolo high tackled him. I don't want to make any excuses but we only get one look at an incident and Tappa Henning, the touch judge, came in immediately. Lomu took the tackle and came up smiling. I'd blown for the penalty and the touch judge advised me it was a yellow card offence. Whilst being supportive of your touch judges you don't have to act on what they tell you if you think differently. I'd seen the incident but I was further away than the touch judge with players crossing in my field of vision. I went along with the touch judge and agreed with him that since it was so early in the game a yellow card would suffice. The game was probably one of the most physical I've been involved in. It was unrelenting. Every tackle was hitting the man hard and fairly, but there was that little bit extra. Tonga rattled the All Blacks who took everything, and the crowd loved it. There was no complaint about how physical it was. Their captain made eyes at me now and again.

The All Blacks came out for the second half having decided to give the Tongans a taste of their own medicine. Later in the game the power of the All Blacks began to tell. They had more left in reserve and Tonga started leaking tries. Then came another incident when the All Blacks reserve scrum half made an outstanding break and was tackled high by Taumalolo. There was a fabulous advantage and the scrum half went on and was brought down a metre from the line. There was criticism later that I could have gone back for the penalty but I felt that the advantage had been taken. The All Blacks had the put in at a scrum a metre from the Tongan line and they scored a try from it. I considered giving Taumalolo another yellow card which would have meant a sending off but my touch judge had had a different view of the incident. I felt the advantage had gone on too far and, although it's difficult, sometimes you have to live by your decisions. It was my responsibility and I decided against the yellow card. Later I discovered that the Match Commissioner did not agree with me.

The game finished and although New Zealand ran out comfortable winners the high score of 45-9 didn't reflect how much Tonga had put in to their game. At the final whistle both sets of players congratulated each other. They had hit hell out of each other during the game but now they were hugging each other. Lomu, who is of Tongan descent, put his arms around his opposing number. We can all learn lessons from that. At the post-match function, the New Zealand captain said the game was exactly what they wanted.

My two assessors were both Irish, Michael Reardon from Limerick and Jim Irvine from Belfast. They hadn't seen a game like it. After the assessment the referee is invited to meet with the assessors and go through the video of the game to discuss things. This was new to me and I had never been into it before. However, I did want to see both high tackling incidents again. We went through it and I received a good mark, particularly for control. That hadn't been much of a problem despite the fierce rucking and mauling and the big hits.

I was now looking forward to my next appointments. The next game was a massive one. I was to be touch judge for England vs New Zealand at Twickenham. The outcome would decide where the teams went. Everyone assumed that either New Zealand or England would top the group. Whoever came second would have to compete in a quarter final play-off. It was my weekend to do 'double-touch' with Tonga vs Italy at Leicester a day later. Peter Marshall from Australia was the referee at Twickenham with Didier Mené of France on the other touch and David McHugh of Ireland as number four. Twickenham was buzzing and was going to be difficult to reach by road. We decided to wait in our little mini-bus outside the England team hotel, which was only half a mile away from ours. We knew that England would have a police escort to the ground, so as they pulled out from their hotel we nipped in behind them and got there with ease

Marshall is a very good referee and was very cool and calm beforehand. He instructed us that he wanted one hundred per cent support from us and he would give us one hundred per cent support in return. He asked us to keep talking to him and that he would be grateful for any help we could give him. The game itself was another tremendously hard affair. For the first twenty minutes England pounded the All Blacks, had many opportunities to score. One huge up-and-under landed right underneath the All Blacks' crossbar and their second row, Robin Brooke jumped and caught it like a full back, formed a ruck and they cleared the decks. Not many second rows could do that. The All Blacks came back with Jonah Lomu again doing quite a bit of damage. There were some unusual tactics. When the All Blacks had a put in at the scrum England played their winger in the back row and placed Lawrence Dallaglio out on the wing marking Lomu in front of me. But the All Blacks countered by rolling off the back of the scrum and gained a lot of ground through this. Peter refereed well and was always in control although he did come in for some boos and whistles from the England crowd when decisions went against them. It was a great occasion and it was a pleasure to be a part of it with the All Blacks winning 30-16. Peter's assessor was a Welshman – Gwyn Watts – and deservedly he had a good report.

The following morning it was off to Leicester for Tonga vs Italy. Again Didier and I were the touch judges with Peter moving to number four and David McHugh in the middle. Tonga had recovered from their match against the All Blacks and this game was nip and tuck. Because both teams had lost their opening matches then whoever lost this one knew they were on their way home. There was a full house and the crowd was magnificent. Tonga won it right at the death by 28-25 and were in celebratory mood.

There was a particular incident at this game which was jumped on by Nick Bunting, who is in charge of the English referees. It was a spitting incident by one of the Italian press. David had always been in control of the game but obviously this member of the Italian media didn't agree and was seen by Nick Bunting. It was a disgusting act. The man was reported and he was sent home the following day. You don't expect that sort of behaviour from anyone let alone members of the media.

We returned to our hotel after the usual post-match function but there was a bombshell waiting for me. It was a telegram from Steve Griffiths of the IRB instructing me to be in Twickenham the following morning for a hearing about an incident during the Tonga vs New Zealand game. The citing commissioner wasn't happy and had called a hearing. The previous week I had been asked to write a report on incidents during the game. It was now quarter to midnight on a Sunday night. I was in Leicester and had to be in Twickenham by nine o'clock the following morning! I phoned Steve in Dublin and told him that it was impossible for me to make it. He understood and asked me to be there as soon as I could. The other officials took my kit and I made my way to Twickenham. I eventually arrived after several tube journeys and a £40 taxi ride across London. The commissioner was a Scottish lawyer. Peter Brown, the former Scottish forward was also on the panel. Taumalolo was also there with the Tongan team manager.

We went through a series of videos and questions from the panel. I felt sorry for Taumalolo, they gave him a grilling. We looked at the incident in slow motion, frame by frame and I was asked if I was happy with my decision to award a yellow card. I told them that I was. There was a second incident involving Taumalolo and Jonah Lomu but it was obvious that the tackle was around Lomu's chest and not dangerous. The third incident we reviewed was the scrum half's break from the base of a scrum at which I had played advantage when he was late tackled. I must admit that it didn't look good on video but they didn't ask me for my opinion on this one, instead they asked Taumalolo to explain his actions. We all left the room and outside I met Colin Charvis who was waiting to go in for his hearing along with Welsh team manager David Pickering. They were on next. It was strange because although Taumalolo is a Tongan, we were all involved with Welsh rugby.

The following day, the news came that Taumalolo had been banned, so had Charvis and the Argentinian prop. It was a new experience for me. For the first time a player that I had not sent off had been banned. It was a very clear message to officials and players alike and, on a personal level, a funny feeling because it felt as though my decisions weren't good enough. I still felt I'd made the correct decision but there was no appeal procedure for the referee if he didn't agree. So we all accepted the hearing panel's findings and got on with the competition. My next set of appointments was another 'double-touch' in Glasgow for South Africa vs Uruguay and the following day in Murrayfield for Scotland vs Spain. Peter Marshall was in the middle for the first game and Clayton Thomas for the latter. My partner on touch was Steve Walsh, then an up and coming youngster from New Zealand. He was nearly half my age and the most annoying thing was that he was fit and good-looking as well! I had heard that he was rather arrogant but I found he had a terrific sense of humour and was great company. He was confident in his own ability and rightly so, but he also loved the game of rugby.

South Africa and Uruguay were to play on a Friday. The previous night we met up with players and officials from Cardiff Rugby Club who were playing in the Welsh-Scottish League. We acknowledged some of the players in the hotel although the greeting from the Cardiff flanker Greg Kacala under his breath was less than pleasant. I had sent him off after ninety seconds in a game at the Gnoll against Neath for an attempted head butt – my fastest sending off. His expletive wasn't in Polish but in perfect English which questioned my parentage; it's nice to know that some players remember you!

We were staying in Edinburgh, so on Friday morning we travelled to Hampden Park in Glasgow for the game. It's a magnificent stadium with a capacity in excess of fifty thousand but there were just two thousand spectators there for South Africa and Uruguay. Questions had already been raised about the pricing of tickets and this was evident with the poor attendance, and this for a game involving the World Champions. Both the attendance and the game were a complete contrast to Peter Marshall's previous match in Twickenham between England and New Zealand. Uruguay got in the faces of South Africa and were a referee's nightmare. One side wants to play rugby and the other just wants to kill it – it is a real recipe for disaster. Frustration set in among the South Africans and in a game where nothing was happening, they had their centre Brendan Venter sent off. Peter hadn't seen the incident, it was called by Steve Walsh on the other touch and to Peter's credit he supported him one hundred per cent. Steve was in no doubt that Venter had to go for stamping. I couldn't wait for a kick at goal to find out what happened. Steve said it was an obvious stamping, out of frustration. In the end South Africa won 39-3 but it was game worthy of just two thousand people.

The next day it was Clayton's game at Murrayfield and thankfully Spain didn't take the same attitude as Uruguay and we had some good rugby with a comfortable win for Scotland. I was pleased for Clayton because his opening match between Ireland and Australia had also involved the citing commissioner suspending players afterwards although he hadn't sent anyone off the field.

I had only been in the middle for one game and a had done a lot as a touch judge so I was anxious to referee again. I now knew what my quarter final play-off fixture was. It was to be England against Fiji at Twickenham and I was anticipating a great game. England were playing some brilliant rugby and if Fiji came out with the correct attitude we would be in for a classic. But after a session in the gym at the hotel in Cardiff, I was approached by Tim Greason, the Chairman of the Appointments Panel who informed me they were changing the fixtures. They wanted to move me to the quarter final in Dublin, which would probably be Ireland vs France. Tim said that since Ireland and France hadn't been at their best discipline-wise they were slightly concerned and wanted me there. It was certainly a compliment. So I would skip a quarter final play-off and would get a full quarter final instead. The other good news was that Clayton was to get the England vs Fiji game and I would be running touch.

England weren't at their best for the game but still won comfortably, 45-24. We returned to the hotel to watch the other quarter final play-off match between Ireland and Argentina. Argentina scored a marvellous try to go ahead and although Ireland pounded the Argentine line they couldn't score and lost narrowly, 28-24. So it was to be Argentina vs France and not Ireland vs France. I felt a little down. I had missed out on a great game between England and Fiji but had felt compensated that I would be doing Ireland vs France in front of a passionate crowd at Lansdowne Road. Suddenly Ireland were out; would anyone be there to watch the game?

Colin Hawke had also been taken from a play-off to referee the quarter final in Cardiff between Wales and Australia. That was the only Saturday match, with the three other matches being played on the Sunday – England vs South Africa in Paris, France vs Argentina in Dublin, with Scotland vs New Zealand at Murrayfield. Unfortunately, my touch judges Brian Campsall and Peter Marshall and I were flying out from Cardiff at about kick off time in the match between Wales and Australia. There was a delay at the airport so we sat in the lounge to watch the game. It was 9-6 to Australia when we were called for the flight. By the time we arrived in Dublin, Australia had won 24-9 and I felt down. Peter wasn't, of course, because Australia were through to the semifinal.

Dublin felt very flat which worsened my feelings. This was to be a World Cup quarter final in Dublin, but without Ireland. We picked up the papers on Sunday morning to find the Irish side and management lambasted. The media were cruel. I'd borne the brunt of some vicious press myself but I hadn't seen anything like this. Ireland had been knocked out of the competition by a side that they were expected to beat and the press really let them know it. But as kick off time approached there was a bit of a build up in atmosphere. I guess the Irish thought that since they'd already bought their tickets, they might as well go along and watch a game of rugby.

We watched Jim referee England vs South Africa on the telly so we knew who two of the semifinalists were before our game began. South Africa had beaten England 44-21, thanks to some prodigious licking by Janie de Beer, who kicked 34 points including a world record five dropped goals. The Dublin kick off was a late one and we had a pleasant surprise when we arrived at Lansdowne Road where there was a crowd of about forty thousand people. I didn't know what to expect in thc game. Grizz Wylie had some concerns about the scrummaging. My concern was that neither side could speak a lot of English which might make it difficult to communicate. Although I'd refereed both sides separately, I'd hadn't done this fixture before. But what a game of rugby! It was end to end stuff. France hit them early and scored some brilliant tries but Argentina came back to within two points at one stage. The crowd didn't seem to be supporting one side more than the other, they seemed just to be supporting rugby. And they got their money's worth.

But since Argentina had to play that extra game in the quarter final play-off they faded in the last quarter of the game. France had had a week between matches to prepare, so they finished the stronger and came through 47-26. Augustin Pichot, the Argentine scrum half was again magnificent and received a standing ovation from the crowd as he went off.

Grizz Wylie told me afterwards that the game was probably ten minutes too long for them. He'd announced before the game that it would be his last as coach to Argentina and he didn't want to end things on a sour note. I had replied that I wouldn't hesitate to red-card any player if the foul warranted it. I promised him however that if a player was giving me any problems I would yellow-card him, which would be a signal to the bench that he should be replaced. The victory over Ireland had really hit the headlines back in Argentina and they didn't want to anything to cloud their achievement. France didn't ask for any similar treatment but I would have done the same for them had they done so. With hindsight I should have mentioned the 'arrangement' with Argentina to the French so they could have done the same had they wished. There was an incident during the game when one of the Argentine props, Mauricio Reggiardi, stiff-arm tackled a French player and I gave him a yellow card. Two minutes later he was sitting on the bench, having been substituted. Grizz was a man of his word. I saw nothing wrong in doing this. The tackle certainly wasn't a sending-off offence.

Things had gone well again and I received a good report from the assessor. So from feeling that this wasn't going to be much of a game I was buzzing again and my thoughts turned to the possibility of another appointment before the end of the tournament. I'd enjoyed working with the other officials, especially Brian Campsall, who is one of the most supportive touch judges you could wish for. With twenty minutes to go he egged me on with "Keep going Bev – only twenty minutes to Guinness time!" He's a superb person but because he's such a supportive touch judge he doesn't get his fair share in the middle.

At the after-match function we watched New Zealand beat Scotland 30-18, so we knew our semifinals. Both were to be played at Twickenham, Australia vs South Africa on the Saturday and France vs New Zealand on the Sunday, and the prediction were for an Australia vs New Zealand final. Although my assessment for the quarter final was good I did think that the Citing Commissioner having over-ruled me in the New Zealand vs Tonga match might count against me. But other officials had also been over-ruled. The appointments were to be made on the Tuesday. But before then we had a Sunday night in Dublin to enjoy and Brian Campsall's company off the field was equal to his support work on it!

We travelled back to Cardiff the following day and the gossip about the appointments started again. We gossip quite a lot, some more than others. It's only natural. In the same way that players have to look out for challengers to their positions, referees look at others who might be vying for the big matches. It's very competitive, though you can enjoy good performances by your colleagues – particularly the Welsh referees. What I don't like is the referee who thrives on the bad performances of others, who draws attention to the mistakes of others but can't see their own. Unfortunately there are one or two individuals like that. But the vast majority appreciate good performances by others, not least because we all know what it's like to have a stinker. We've all felt at the end of the game that we wish we could turn the clock back and have another go at it.

Back in Cardiff I was horrified to see the reaction of the Welsh media, and indeed the public, towards Colin Hawke, who'd refereed Wales vs Australia. I'd only heard snippets about the game and the Irish newspapers had been so busy berating their own team there wasn't much written about the Welsh game. I spoke with friends and with other officials who told me that the abuse directed towards Colin was horrendous. It was totally over the top. I managed to speak with him and he was really down. He's a lovely bloke and has a wicked sense of humour. But after the game he was told he'd be given a police escort from the ground to the hotel, nearby. Expectations were far too high in Wales and the team's performances in the pool matches certainly weren't of the quality to win the World Cup. Colin certainly knew he'd under-performed but he was also taken aback by the reaction. His assessor was Jim Irvine. He's a very honest man and it wasn't a good one. Colin is highly rated throughout world rugby. He'd been given a real compliment by being taken from one game in the competition to deal with a more difficult fixture. But the reaction didn't stop on the Monday: it continued all week. In our hotel there was a reading room where we could relax. All the newspapers were there, as well as videos. Seeing them daily affected Colin really badly. He didn't want to leave the hotel and spent a lot of time in his room. He even ate there alone rather than go out to a restaurant. I invited him out for a drink but he even declined that because he feared that someone would have a go at him and things would turn nasty. When he realized that he wouldn't be involved in the remaining matches, he went to London for a few days just to get out of Wales. I don't think I've seen anyone as down as he was – he was almost a broken man. All this because of a game of rugby. Everyone is open to criticism out in the middle if things don't go well but what happened to Colin was totally unjustified.

We all had our tips for the remaining matches. I had no expectation for the final because of 1991. I still believed the committee wouldn't give two finals to anyone. But once again the draw meant that I could be considered for either of the two semis or the third place play-off. The minimum I hoped for was running touch. There were limitations on some referees. New Zealand referees always suffer because their team is always successful. Their worst performance has been a semifinal, although they'd only won the World Cup once. Paddy O'Brien, on his own admission, had let himself down in the Fiji vs France game and Colin Hawke didn't expect to be involved. Paul Honiss was an up and coming referee but probably not experienced enough to take on these matches. So this opened it up a bit more. We were trying to forecast who would win the matches so we could anticipate the appointments.

There was a different system of appointing for the final stages of the competition. This time the assessors weren't involved in the selection of match officials as they had been in previous tournaments. Tuesday morning arrived and my tip for the final was Jim Fleming. His performance in the England vs South Africa quarter final had been outstanding. He ran himself into the ground and even got under the posts for the dropped-goals as well – lucky for him he'd chosen the bleep fitness test. It was also his fourth World Cup and he might get his reward. So he really didn't want his name to come out when the semis were awarded. We all gathered in the hotel to hear the news. There were only eight officials to be announced so it didn't take much time. The first game was Australia vs South Africa on the Saturday and my name was announced to referee, with Chris White of England and Clayton running touch and Joel Dumé of France as number four. Then came the Sunday semi and the first name out was Jim Fleming. I looked at him and though he'd just been selected to referee a World Cup semifinal he seemed massively disappointed. He couldn't hide it and I felt for him. He knew he wouldn't get the final.

Naturally I was delighted with my game. It was probably the only option open to me. While I would have been happy with the third place play-off, a semifinal is ten times better. Despite the winners getting automatic qualification for the next World Cup, we haven't had a good third place game yet: it's difficult to motivate players in the shadow of the impending final. Jim and I went out on our own for a few beers on the night of the appointments and by the end of the night I'd managed to convince him that it was a big honour and a compliment for him and that he was still young enough to get a final of his own. He was back on track and determined to do well.

I was preparing now not only for my last World Cup match but possibly my last international. I didn't know if I would be involved in the Six Nations campaign. If the IRB were planning ahead then perhaps they would want to give more experience to referees who would be involved in the World Cup 2003. So I might be surplus to requirements. We all went up to London on Friday, the day before our game in Twickenham. The eight 'active' officials were put in one hotel but the others were sent elsewhere to enjoy themselves for the whole weekend. The four of us involved in the Saturday game would then join in on Sunday.

It had been quite an active week in the build-up and I had begun to think about the game. I reflected on the same stage four years previously and that downpour in Durban. We also started talking about the other two matches. Now that my favourite for the final wouldn't be there I mulled over who would get it. New Zealand were hot tips for the final and I believed that the outcome of our game would determine the appointment. The main referees from the northern hemisphere would have previously refereed the final or a semifinal, so I guessed it would be someone from the southern hemisphere – Peter Marshall, of Australia, if South Africa got through or Andre Watson from South Africa, if Australia went through. It is an awkward situation for a referee. Naturally you want your country to go through and you would be bitterly disappointed if they didn't, but dismay would soon turn to elation if you were selected for the final. You would have to be a very selfish person to put your own gratification before success for your country.

My semifinal was another immense occasion. I hadn't felt so much pressure since the opening match of the 1995 tournament. Twickenham saw the best rugby of the tournament and that weekend it saw two matches in complete contrast to each other in style but equally intriguing. The ground was full and we didn't have a try. The game seemed to go on and on and I thought that there would only be one score in it at the end. Both captains were outstanding, as was the discipline. There were calls for a penalty try from the Australians when the ball hit a South African who was retreating from an offside position. I gave a penalty and the South Africans thought it was a harsh decision against them. This is what you get on the field when both sides are desperate for points. The pressure was on me to ensure that every decision I gave was the correct one. Penalties were at a premium and both place kickers were doing well. When you make a mistake when it's 25-0 nobody really cares, apart from yourself, it doesn't really influence the result. But a mistake in such a close and important game would have serious repercussions. Every decision you make is scrutinized by the players, coaches, public and pundits with their slow motion replays. Not only are honesty and fair play important factors, but the referee's character must be able to take it.

The match itself was like nothing I'd been involved in before. Questions were raised about the amount of injury time I'd allowed, but in refereeing terms there's no such thing as 'injury time', it's all 'playing time'. The Australian assistant coach joked then that I must be wearing my Louis Luyt watch. For the first time in a match under my control an official held up a board for the crowd to see how much time was left to play in addition to the regulation forty minutes. This is done 'down under' and in South Africa they now use a klaxon. The southern hemisphere referees are familiar with raising their hand whenever there's a stoppage to signal to the time-keeper to stop the clock. The referee then puts his arm up again for the signal to restart the clock. We were advised to do this during the tournament. I'd been refereeing for twenty-seven years and I had never done this before, so sometimes I was doing it and sometimes I wasn't – which made it difficult for the sideline officials to calculate the injury time. All the northern hemisphere referees had difficulty with the signalling: we just weren't used to it.

However, I had my two watches and also Clayton and Chris had theirs. We had decided between us that the next time the ball went dead the match would be over. But the ball didn't go dead, I awarded a penalty against Australia. We were now in the forty-fifth minute of the half. It was a difficult kick and de Beer had to go for it. At the time the score was 18-15 to Australia and the match would be over after the kick. What a pressure kick: he put it right between the posts. I blew the whistle for the successful kick and immediately blew again for full time. We all marched off to the dressing room to prepare for extra time. I told the players they had five minutes before starting again.

In the dressing room Clayton and Chris said they were also feeling the pressure because they could signal for an offence which would also have a bearing on the outcome. But despite the pressure we were all loving every bloody second of it. This is what you dream of as an official, to be involved in a big game in a big arena during the biggest tournament of all – there's nothing like it. Referees must be masochists! And we were going back out for another ten minutes each way. Even though I'd struggled to pass the pre-tournament fitness test my adrenaline alone would ensure I'd get through twenty minutes of extra time. The team managers from both sides were nervously confirming the tournament rules in the event of the scores being level after extra time had been played. South Africa's disciplinary record was poorer than that of the Australians. Their centre had been sent off in that nothing game against Uruguay and the dismissal could again prove crucial.

But that wasn't going through my mind at all at the time. I had to keep my concentration and focus on the game being played in front of me. The crowd had returned to their seats from their 'comfort' break and the atmosphere was electric. Australia managed to score one goal more than South Africa and squeezed through to the final. The last twenty minutes were as tense as the first eighty. I was also happy that my own performance didn't diminish. In fact I was even more resolute. The players depended on me to referee in the same way throughout the match. They knew what I was giving and what I was allowing, so to change my refereeing in the last twenty minutes would be letting them down. There were substitutions and fresh legs on both sides, and Stephen Larkham, the Australian outside half, dropped a remarkable goal completely out of the blue. Normally you can see when an outside half is lining up and I'm usually on my way to the posts. But this one caught me out: he just kicked it and the ball just went and went, over the crossbar and there was a terrific roar from the crowd. There was a further exchange of penalties but then for

Australia it was a case of retaining possession.

Both John Eales and Joost van der Westhuizen kept looking at me and asking me how much time was left. I thought it was fair that I said we were moving into the very little bit of injury time. There's nothing wrong with telling both captains the same. We had one team wanting to put the ball dead and one trying to keep the ball alive. Australia were awarded a penalty and booted the ball right into the stand. I blew the whistle and it was all over, 27-21 to Australia. George Gregan, the Australian scrum half, ran up to me and said "Was that some f****** game of rugby!"

I went into the dressing room and I was absolutely knackered. There was now a challenge to France and New Zealand: 'Beat this if you can!' Rod McQueen, the Australian coach, was naturally a happy man and he came in to thank us, and so did John Eales. But the nice part was that Nick Mallett, the Springboks coach, also came to see us. He put his arms around me and said, "It's been a long day". He had no complaints. His team had just missed out on the World Cup Final and had lost the trophy his South Africa had won four years ago. He had to face the third place play-off, but he still came in to thank us. It was the action of a big man and spoke volumes of his character. Even at this level, there was still a lot of humility.

The World Cup was now over for me – or was it? I had never officiated at the Millennium Stadium and I thought how nice it would be to run the line in either of the two remaining games. But I realised that I was being rather greedy. I'd had marvellous appointments throughout my World Cup career so a part of me felt I shouldn't expect more. I enjoyed myself that night and I had Sunday to look forward to and a seat for New Zealand vs France. In the stand I sat next to Joel Dumé. He had his flags and before the match he said he hoped France wouldn't embarrass us. It appeared that any neutral in the ground was supporting France. There were Welshmen, Scotsmen, Englishmen and Irishmen all cheering for France. New Zealand have great support wherever they go but they were completely outnumbered by those who were French for the day. It was an amazing place to be. We were all shouting "Allez Bleu!"

As the game went on and everyone realised they were witnessing one of THE greatest games of rugby, Joel kept saying, "Derek, pinch me. It's fantastique, I must be dreaming!" The previous day, we had penalties and dropped goals but here we had fantastic tries and the All Blacks being cut down to size. What a weekend. Twickenham – you lucky bastards! Australia were going into the Final having conceded just one try but instead of being up against New Zealand, the old enemy who they knew so well, they would be facing the unpredictable French. But France had upset the form book and put John Hart on the dole, so if they could do it to the All Blacks could they also do it to the Wallabies?

So it was back to Cardiff for the announcement of the officials. We had the prospect of a South Africa vs New Zealand play-off – a repeat of the 1995 World Cup Final. Cardiff was buzzing and people from all over the world were arriving for the two remaining matches. I'd made my mind up that the referee for the Final would be Andre Watson. It was no surprise that Peter Marshall was selected to be in charge of the play-off. And thirty seconds after that came Andre's confirmation. It was a massive step up for him but also an indication of the confidence the selectors had in him. So there were six of us left with no involvement. I had no complaints because over four World Cups the selectors had been more than generous to me and in return I don't think that I had let them down. But I'd come to the end.

Although the third place play-off is always an anti-climactic game to play in, if you tell a South African that it's an opportunity to beat the All Blacks, then it's a different proposition. In fairness, both sets of supporters turned out in force and the victory for South Africa meant fourth place was New Zealand's lowest placing in the four World Cups. They won in 1987, were third in 1991, and lost in the 1995 final. And they consider that to be failure. It's ironic that a New Zealand official could have refereed the final but both Paddy and Colin had not had the best of tournaments.

The Final itself proved a difficult one to referee. It never seemed to get going. Maybe another referee on another day would have let it run a bit more. Andre is a talker. It's his style, which has proved to be successful for him. France couldn't repeat their semifinal performance and Australia won the World Cup 35-12. It was their second win and they ended the tournament still with only one try scored against them. They had played Ireland, Wales, South Africa and France and hadn't conceded a try against them. The United

States were the only side to cross their line. They'd had the best defence throughout and never looked like losing the Final – they were worthy champions.

Cups

As a player I was fortunate to play against the British Lions centre Arthur Lewis when Vardre entertained Ebbw Vale in an early round of the Welsh Challenge Cup. It was a big thrill for the Vardre, the sort of match which highlights the romance of the cup competition. It's sad nowadays that the big clubs do not enter the cup until the latter stages which deprives many of the small village clubs of a day to remember and a significant financial boost.

One of the first cup matches I was involved in was a round of the 1980 Schweppes Cup, as the Welsh Challenge Cup was known then. It was a match which is still talked about today – Penclawdd vs Newport, a real David and Goliath encounter. It was an awful day: we'd had about forty eight hours of continuous rain, which Penclawdd probably saw as being a great leveller. Newport at that particular time weren't having a very impressive season. I received a phone call on the morning of the match from the Secretary of Penclawdd informing me that the game was definitely going ahead, which surprised me since I lived not that far away. Normally if the pitch was in a dreadful condition the home club Secretary would phone the referee and the away side so they wouldn't have to travel. But if the match was local, upon arrival the referee would decide if the pitch was playable, the safety of the players being his prime consideration.

Other cup matches throughout south Wales were being cancelled by the minute during the morning, and our fixture was one of the few remaining by the afternoon. When I arrived in Penclawdd I immediately inspected the pitch, and there was no question about the state of the ground. I had started matches in far worse conditions so everything appeared to be fine. The match went down in history. The Penclawdd number eight, Kevin Dallimore, scored the only try of the game by charging down a kick, and the minnows of Penclawdd had beaten one of the most famous clubs in rugby 4-0. At the final whistle their hooker picked me up and kissed me. The following day the press commented that they had seen referees criticised before, even praised, but they hadn't seen one kissed! The Penclawdd clubhouse ran out of beer after the game. In fairness to Newport they took the defeat extremely well and they stayed on for quite a while after the match, which showed good sportsmanship. A few years later Dallimore had transferred to Dunvant and when I saw him in the changing room before refereeing them in a cup match against Pontypridd he remarked how nice it would be if the score could be the same again. Incredibly it was a shock win for Dunvant with only one try in the game and no penalties or conversions.

My first final was between Cardiff and Llanelli in 1985. This was the first time that there would be live television coverage of the final – but only the second half. I was pleased with this because I didn't get to grips with the match in the first half. I had tremendous problems with the front rows. After about half an hour I was being slow handclapped by the crowd. It's very difficult when you've got six men, most of them international players, who've got their own personal battles going on during a game. Here were Lawrence Delaney, Ceri Townley and Anthony Buchanan from Llanelli against Jeff Whitefoot, Alan Phillips and Ian Eidman. They really went at each other. Front row play is notoriously difficult to read and if you're on one side of the scrum then they're messing about on the other and vice versa. I was giving a lot of penalties and using a lot of the whistle but to be quite honest I wasn't sure if I was penalizing the correct man. But by half time everything had sorted itself out and both front rows decided they'd be better employed playing good rugby. By the time the television coverage started if was quite a good game.

It went down to the wire and in the dying moments Llanelli had a scrum and the ball went out to their outside half, Gary Pearce, who put over a dropped goal to win the game. Cardiff certainly weren't happy with my performance and thought that I'd misread the scrummaging and that they were far superior to Llanelli in this facet and that I was protecting the Llanelli front row.

Perhaps because of the first half I had to wait three years for my next final, between Llanelli and Neath in 1988. This was a notorious game because Jonathan Davies, who had gone to Llanelli from Neath, had received a lot of so-called 'hate-mail', and there had been a lot of quite unsavoury build-up to the match. It was another tough game and very physical. Llanelli scored a try quite early on and after that Neath were always chasing the game, although they were never out of it. The Neath back row tried to hound Jonathan and I had to keep a close watch on them. But Jonathan had the last laugh and Llanelli won the Cup.

My third Cup Final involved Llanelli again, this time against Pontypool in 1991. Pooler had David Bishop in their team and the first half was a torrid affair as they pounded the Llanelli line. Llanelli held out, the game opened up in the second half and they were convincing winners. So my first three finals saw a hat-trick of wins for Llanelli.

My last Cup Final came after a five year gap. A lot of promising young referees were coming on the scene so it was good for them to have their opportunity. The match was between Neath and Pontypridd. My touch judges were Robert Davies and Clayton Thomas. Normally for a final the officials arrive at the ground two hours before the kick off. I began getting into my kit with about three quarters of an hour to kick off but there was no sign of the touch judges. They still hadn't turned up half an hour later and it was now time to inspect the players' boots, which the touch judges are also involved in. I did this on my own and also the toss up. We now had only fifteen minutes to go, and could see we had to do something about it. First, we found a current referee in the crowd – Ken Rowlands' nephew Allan Ware – and then got hold of Bob Yemen, who had retired from refereeing. They had to borrow kit. With five minutes to go we were given the cue from the television people to go on to the pitch when a panic-stricken Robert Davies and Clayton Thomas arrived. They were full of sweat. They had decided to travel to Cardiff by train and had been stuck in some sidings! Clayton was cursing because he hates being late. I couldn't stand out in the middle on my own so while Rob and Clayton got changed the 'replacement' touch judges came out with me. They were there through the anthems and the team introductions. Just before I blew the whistle to start the game Rob and Clayton burst out of the dressing room and took their places. Allan, the touch judge on the far side, was urging me to kick off so that he could officiate! (His contribution to rugby became notable a few years later when he refereed the rebel matches involving Cardiff and Swansea against teams from England. He even sent off Bath's Victor Ubogu in a match against Cardiff at the Arms Park.)

Neath threw the final away. For a long time they were on top and then Pontypridd came back to win it in the final quarter. Neath made up for it by beating Pontypridd the following week and clinching the League. They won the title by pipping Cardiff on try count. Strangely enough I was refereeing Cardiff that same night in their home match against Llanelli. I work with a lot of Neath people and they'd been teasing me to keep the try scoring down!

I actually played for Neath, one game back at the end of the seventies and Neath must have been short of players! They asked some of us from west Wales to play for them against London Welsh, who had the great Gerald Davies in their line-up. The players they had meant I wasn't just out of my league but off the planet ability-wise. At one point I was running across to tackle Gerald and believe it or not I got there too soon! I thought he could easily cut inside me but as I eased off he accelerated and I was grasping fresh air! There's quite a good view of the Gnoll from behind the posts and that's where we spent most of the game as London Welsh crushed us.

The European Cup

The appointments to European Cup matches were exactly like those for an international. Referees had to be neutral and from countries other than those competing in a particular fixture. You were graded in each game by assessors and your marks in the pool matches decided whether or not you would be considered for the later knock-out stages. The competition was a massive step up for referees from club rugby and provided a great testing ground for some to further their ambitions. Of course, a poor performance could have the opposite effect. The most notable year for me was 1997, by which I mean the second half of the 1996-97 season and the first part of 1997-98.

I wasn't among the officials for the semifinals in 1996-97 and had to wait to see who came through. As it was a Leicester vs Brive final I was in with a shout. The previous final had been between Cardiff and Toulouse, with an Irish referee, so this year the odds were on a choice between the Welsh and the Scots, and thankfully the Welsh won. That the final was to be played in the National Stadium in Cardiff was a further factor in our favour.

Leicester had a very good side, including the young Austin Healey and Will Greenwood, the entire England front row of Cockerill, Garforth and Rowntree, Martin Johnson in the second row and Dean Richards at number eight. Brive had some great names too: Lamaison, Kacala and Penaud. The match itself was a cracker. Brive had brought about 15,000 supporters with them and Leicester, England's best supported side, had about 25,000 there. The French had come with bands, hooters and horns and were very, very noisy. Bob Dwyer was coach of Leicester and like most Australians is never short of a few words: he was providing some of the Leicester noise. Dean Richards was their captain. I'd first met him when he was playing for English Police against Welsh Police in Bridgend. Wade Dooley played with him. Richards was very young but he had huge potential. He's got a great sense of humour and would crack a joke during a game as well as being serious. But he loved to play the game at his own pace! He had the great ability to read the game well and to do the right thing at the right time. You could talk to him on the field and he would listen. He was never nasty or over-critical but he did tell you if he didn't agree with you.

In the final Richards wanted rucks and mauls and the French wanted the ball in their hands at every opportunity so there was the prospect of a real clash of styles. Brive had a flying winger called Carat and they to get the ball out to him as much as possible. Unfortunately Leicester decided to run the ball when the game was over and Brive had clinched it. As the Leicester players were lining up to receive their runners-up medal Austin Healey passed comment to me that I'd get another gold watch for my performance, but from the French this time. Austin is never short of a few words; I just reminded him to make sure he got his runners-up medal. But we've had some fun times since then. He's got a wicked sense of humour and probably speaks out of turn more times than he should, but then again he's a person I like. He's got this wonderful ability of rubbing his opponents up the wrong way so they concentrate on nailing him, allowing him to free up other players. Bob Dwyer reluctantly admitted they were outplayed, but he took the opportunity to criticize my refereeing of the lineout. Looking back over the match I was very pleased with my performance, but if there was a part of the game where I was open to criticism then Dwyer was probably correct.

In September of the following season, 1997-98, I went down to the French club Bourgoin for their pool match against Harlequins. The Quins had Keith Wood and Gareth Llewellyn in their line up along with the two Frenchmen, Thierry Lacroix and Laurent Cabannes. It was an outstanding game of rugby and the lead changed hands several times. Harlequins just pipped them, 30-18, with Cabannes scoring two tries in the last ten minutes which also earned him a recall into the French squad. I also refereed Harlequins in France again, this time in November for their quarter final in Toulouse. The Quins had many seasoned internationals in their squad but found the Toulouse and France winger Emile N'Tmack in outstanding form. He scored two scintillating tries early on which enhanced Toulouse's position as tournament favourites. They went on to win the match easily, 51-10, in one of the best club performances I've seen. Then, in December, I went to Bath for their semifinal against Pau, which Bath won 20-14. So, in the calendar year I'd refereed a full house of pool matches, a quarter final, semifinal and the final of the European Cup.

The Five and Six Nations

Having refereed my first Five Nations fixture between France and England, which was my first *big* international, in 1986, I then had to wait five years before being appointed to my second. At that time there were a few changes on the Welsh Referees' International Panel. Clive and myself were there and Winston lost his place to Ken then Ken lost it back to Winston and Winston then lost it to Les. So the WRU would have wanted to give everyone a game over that period. There were no IRB appointments then and Clive was considered to be the number one Welsh referee so he had most fixtures. When a new man, such as Les, comes along, then it makes sense for him to be given a few games otherwise there's no point him being on the Panel. But my lack of Five Nations appointments during time were part of a learning process for me as a referee.

I've never tried to emulate another referee's style, I'm definitely my own man. What works for Clive Norling and Winston Jones might not work for Derek Bevan. Likewise what works for me may not suit someone else. I've got my own manner in talking to the players – I've heard some international referees speak to players and have been appalled. I couldn't speak with players and use foul language all the time, it's unnecessary. When you're running the line you do get a close look at the referee and hear what he's saying to players. When decisions are made in the middle you consider whether or not you would have given that particular decision or reacted in that way or differently. Sometimes you don't agree with the referee. Is the referee making the correct decisions? Is he losing control? Is there anything I can do to help him? In your early days as a touch judge, these are the things that go through your mind. But if you try to copy another referee you'll lose something that may be unique to you. Some referees who move up the ladder feel that they must change as they become more successful. That's sad; you're receiving promotion because the powers-that-be like what they see. So why change? And it's very dangerous to reach the top and then believe there's nothing further to learn. It's too easy to become big for your boots, and you can disappear down the ladder just as quickly as you move up it. There was a question mark against the standard of my refereeing on my return from the 1987 World Cup, and rightly so. The WRU's appointments panel couldn't justify selecting me for a Five Nations fixture. My non-selection was a way of bringing me back down to earth because my domestic form wasn't good.

Ironically, my second Five Nations fixture came in 1991, the same year that I was appointed to referee the World Cup Final. I had been on many tours in the meantime – to New Zealand twice, Australia and Japan. In 1991 my Five Nations' fixture was Ireland against France in Dublin. I'd spent five weeks with Ireland in Japan so they knew me and I knew them pretty well by then. I've never made any secret of the fact that I love Dublin, the atmosphere of Lansdowne Road and the attitude of the people. Lansdowne Road may not be the greatest stadium in the world but certainly the warmth of the welcome is the best. The team itself always seems to be the friendliest, though not for the eighty minutes of the game. But before and after the game things are totally different. With some teams the welcome after the game they have lost isn't so warm. But the Irish, win or lose, are the same. They certainly have their say and the coach will tell you exactly what he thinks, but then it's forgotten.

I certainly enjoyed the company of the Ireland team in Japan, early on in my international career. It was the year that they had won the championship and I was on touch for their game against France and the late Kerry Fitzgerald was the referee. Winston was the other touch judge. Japan had asked Ireland to bring with them a British referee. The Irish manager approached me in the hotel on the morning of their match against France and asked me whether I would be interested in touring Japan with them. Naturally I was thrilled and jumped at the chance but I was sworn to secrecy! I couldn't even tell Winston! But I had to say something to him because I was so excited to receive the invitation.

The game itself was a real blood and thunder affair, and Kerry had his hand full. Both captains, Philippe Dintrans of France and Ciaran Fitzgerald of Ireland, were at each others throats. There were six 'flagging' incidents during the game. Winston 'flagged' three times against Ireland and I 'flagged' three times against France. Dintrans came up to me after the game and said, "You go to Japan with Ireland – I think so after today!" Winston had told him: he could never keep a secret! I certainly wasn't offended by the comment; I was going to Japan for five weeks so I didn't care.

So in 1991 I was back at Lansdowne Road for Ireland against France but this time in the middle. France won the game 21-13 and it was a good one to referee. It was World Cup year, there had been nothing controversial and the French played some cracking rugby. It was a stepping stone for me although I came off the field not entirely happy with my performance. It was always difficult for me to referee Ireland. They had some great players such as Willie Anderson, Donal Lenihan, Hugo MacNeill, Brendan Mullin, Michael Kiernan, Philip Matthews and Ollie Campbell. The Irish thought that I was harder on them because I knew them so well. They always called me 'Bev'. I didn't particularly like that, I much prefer 'ref'. During one pre-match briefing before a Tri-Nations match which Ed Morrison was refereeing, the Australians didn't like Ed calling the New Zealand players by their first names. But Ed referred to every player he knew by their first names, then he would use numbers. That's his style and it was very petty of Australia to bring that up. Ed must have put in some excellent performances if that was the only thing they could bring up.

Ireland seem to get it right. They very rarely complain about the referee. Instead they look at the reasons why they were penalised and try to put things right. You mustn't change your style to suit the teams. As a referee you have been selected because you've been successful. So if you are influenced by the teams and their coaches then you will lose something. But these days coaches will look back at the referee's performance over previous matches to judge what they can get away with and what they can't. They will look at the strengths and weaknesses of a referee. A touring team will ask for a complete list of the referees.

Les Peard richly deserved all his appointments and refereed one of the finest matches in which I've had the pleasure of running touch. It was England against France at Twickenham in 1991. Clive and I were under the posts as England attempted a penalty. I'm more nervous behind the posts for a kick at goal than at any other time during a game, even when I'm refereeing. I hate it because some of the kicks are so difficult to judge. The kick skimmed the posts and missed. I screamed across to Clive: "NO". Serge Blanco, the French full back, caught the ball behind me. As touch judges we had instructions to stay where we were until the ball went dead. Blanco had options: he could open it out, kick to touch or minor the ball. What he didn't want was a touch judge running in front of him. So we stayed put. He looked up. England were waiting for him to minor the ball but off he went down the field from behind his own line. The French were gone and I was galloping back to my touch line to try to keep up. I ran as fast as I could but had only reached the ten metre line when the French winger Phillippe Saint-André was scoring a try at the other end. Clive had stayed still the same as me so we were both gasping for breath as we headed for the English posts. Les had actually caught up with play but he was in a similar state near the French kicker. It was an exhilarating try! Despite that, however, England won 21-19 and, in the process, took their first Grand Slam for eleven years.

Within the Five, and now Six, Nations Tournament, the Calcutta Cup games between England and Scotland are always something to savour. The greatest one, in my opinion, was when Les Peard and I ran touch for David Bishop at Murrayfield in 1990, which was a Grand Slam decider for both teams. England were firm favourites and everyone thought it would be a formality for them. Led by Will Carling the England players ran out waving to their friends and families in the crowd. There was then a short delay before the Scotland team walked out slowly, full of determination, led by their captain, David Sole. It was an incredible moment and the crowd immediately sensed something special was about to happen. Scotland had won the game before they'd even kicked a ball. England's tactics helped. I couldn't understand why, although they were awarded lots of penalties, they chose not to kick at goal. It probably cost them the game as Scotland won 13-7. For tension, I haven't experienced another Five Nations match like it. Things boiled over at the after-match function and there wasn't good order for the speeches – there'd been some problems in the front row during the game. I've spoken to international front row players and there are times when even they don't know who's responsible. As a referee you don't like to guess, but sometimes you have to play the averages. There'd been a lot of collapsed scrums and the drink was flowing quite a lot at the dinner, which didn't help.

My first Calcutta Cup in the middle was in 1992, at Murrayfield again, when England got the revenge for losing the Grand Slam by winning 25-7. It was a very settled England side which was starting its era of dominance with Dewi Morris, Rob Andrew and Jerry Guscott. I was back in the middle at Murrayfield in 1996 for a game which was memorable for a different reason. Les Peard was one of the touch judges, who were now allowed to 'flag' for offences. Les did just that and I went over to speak with him. There was sound recordist running alongside his cameraman as I arrived and our conversation came over the airwaves and loud and clear. "Trampling by an English forward, but I'm sorry I haven't got his f******* number!" said Les. To make matters worse his wife and daughter were watching the television back home. Les is a policeman and although he took a lot of ribbing I believe he also got a ticking off from his Chief Constable. But I do sympathise because it's easy to do, and he's been known as 'Effin Les' ever since.

Each venue in the Five Nations had a different atmosphere. Unfortunately, of course, I could never savour the atmosphere in Cardiff for a Welsh game as a referee. Lansdowne Road, as I have said, is my favourite ground. Murrayfield was a great place. I preferred the old stadium because now, since the redevelopment there's a big gap on one side due to the running track. I'm rather old fashioned and like the crowd as near as possible to the pitch. It gives a game far more atmosphere. Twickenham is a fabulous stadium. The roar of the crowd seems to hit the roof and bounce back down again. The atmosphere there is great. I refereed in a Varsity game there in 1993 and although the standard of the match is no greater than a mediocre club game the students make quite a bit of noise.

Although I didn't get the pleasure of refereeing at the new Stade de France, I have run touch there and also at the old Stade Colombes. All my matches in the middle were at Parc des Princes, with the exception of one international between France and South Africa in Lyon. I recall in 1993 there was a very close victory for France over Scotland, during which I suffered from food poisoning. Gareth Simmonds, Bob Yemen and myself were the officials and we had a torrid time. We all went out for a meal the night before the game and I awoke in the early hours with food poisoning. I was vomiting and I had diarrhoea and this continued all through the night. I saw a doctor first thing in the morning and he gave me some tablets. And as we'd travelled to France together we found out that Gareth was suffering with severe piles! He was in real pain during the game and since he was the number one touch judge, he begged me to last until the final whistle. Bob hadn't refereed an international yet. Somehow between my sickness and Gareth's piles we got through the game. I've never felt so ill during a match. Bob phoned home afterwards and his wife thought we all looked well on the television!

That was certainly an appointment I was pleased to get through and get back home. This might be an appropriate time to mention the welcome home I received from my club Vardre after international matches. For a long time the clubhouse was just a basic affair. We were one of the first in the area to have our own clubhouse, which we built out of wood and christened 'The Shed'. We later bought a pub which we converted along with land for pitches. When you have a clubhouse you also need to decorate the walls with rugby memorabilia, and I was asked to furnish a picture of myself in my international referees' jersey. This was duly placed on the wall but the members added a toilet seat as a frame. Whenever I came back from an international game the picture was the first thing I looked for. If the lid of the toilet seat was up and I could see myself, then I knew the boys thought I'd had a good game. But if the lid was down then I knew that I'd had a stinker! I didn't need an assessors report: the toilet seat said it all. Thankfully the lid was more up than down.

My last Five Nations match was another Murrayfield fixture, this time between Scotland and Ireland in the season leading up to the World Cup in 1999. Clive told me it was the 'kiss of death' – a notoriously hard and boring match. But it turned out to be one of the best games I've had the pleasure to referee, and really put me in contention for my fourth World Cup. There'd been problems in the front row in almost all of Ireland's games during the championship. I was a little worried beforehand about what I would say to them before the game. Front row players can make or break a referee but I decided to say nothing to them. I went in to check the studs of the Scottish team and I didn't say a word to their front row. I then did the same with the Irish team. Their front row was Wallace, Wood and Clohessy. They walked towards me and asked me whether or not I wanted to speak with them. I said that I didn't and asked them why they thought I might. Wallace said that during the three previous internationals the referee had told them how to scrummage! "Well you didn't bloody listen to them," I replied, and walked out of the dressing room. They were dumbfounded and I didn't have any problems with them during the game. So with a good foundation in the scrummage and both sides wanting to play rugby I was on to a winner.

The Tri-Nations

The atmosphere in the Tri-Nations involving South Africa, Australia and New Zealand is very different. The competition started in 1996, so it is quite a new one, without the history and tradition of our Five Nations. But these three countries, of course, have a lot of history in playing each other, but not within a structured competition. The Kiwis hate losing to the Aussies in the way we in Wales hate losing to England. The depth of feeling between South Africa and New Zealand is amazing. The standard and intensity of rugby in the competition is higher than in Europe and the Tri-Nations is regarded as the jewel of appointments for a referee. The build-up in the media to one of these matches is massive and starts weeks before a game is played. I would get dozens of phone calls in my hotel from the media asking for comment. I would be asked "Do you know that you've refereed the All Blacks to more defeats than any other referee? Will you adopt the same attitude in this game?" Although the fact is true, how can you answer such a crazy question?

I refereed the All Blacks on tour in South Africa in 1996 when they played a three match test rubber. They were two-nil up and I was in the middle for the third test in Johannesburg. Although the All Blacks had already wrapped up the series it wasn't good enough for them because they wanted a white – or 'blackwash' as they called it. It was a year after the Boks had beaten the All Blacks in the final of the World Cup, so New Zealand was out for revenge. South Africa, meanwhile, were determined to redeem themselves in the series. The game was notable for a man-of-the-match performance by Andre Joubert, the Springboks' full back. He was absolutely outstanding and scored a scintillating try in South Africa's 33-22 win. John Hart, the New Zealand coach, wasn't happy with my refereeing and told me that he was glad it hadn't been one apiece in the series. I asked him to be more specific but unfortunately he wouldn't or couldn't go in to detail – he just said it was my overall performance. To me that meant there was nothing he could pick on. He crossed swords with me a few times, but he seemed to be upset by any referee who was involved in an All Black defeat. Coaches, particularly ones who've just seen their team lose, shouldn't say much right at the end of the game when their disappointment is high. But the media must always have immediate comment, particularly if there's a hint of controversy. I always checked with my touch judges after a game and demanded complete honesty from them to see if there was something I'd missed or whether my performance had been lacking. I think I was quite a good judge of my own performance so if something wasn't as it should have been, normally I didn't need anyone to tell me.

Murray Mexted, the former All Black number eight, now commentates for television in New Zealand, and seems to have something against me. His comment as the Tri-Nations match between New Zealand and South Africa in Auckland in 1997 was kicking off was: "The referee today is Derek Bevan of Wales so we know what to expect today: whistle, whistle, whistle." Ed Morrison and myself don't seem to be among his favourites. This may stem from some pique on Mexted's part because Ed and I refused to be interviewed by him before a game in New Zealand. He just appeared at our hotel without prior arrangement expecting us to be interviewed. It wasn't convenient for us so he had to leave with his tail between his legs. Maybe that's the root of it. I'm not a fan of his commentary, he lacks knowledge of the laws and because he can't debate decisions looks for controversy and takes cheap shots at the referee. He was a great player, but as a commentator he doesn't match up.

It was in that game that I had to send off my first player in a Tri-Nations game, in fact the only player I ever sent off in an international – Andre Venter, the South African flanker. The game was fast, open and attacking. There was nothing in it at half time and about eight minutes into the second half Sean Fitzpatrick was caught at the bottom of a ruck. Venter came in and stamped on his head. I had no hesitation in reaching for the red card. I could see he was devastated. He's a real proud South African and he knew he'd let down his team mates and his country. It's difficult enough to play against New Zealand with fifteen men; with only fourteen it's nigh on impossible. The All Blacks won comfortably, 55-35, and I received one of my best refereeing assessments Down Under. John Hart had no complaints that day and neither did South Africa. I had to attend the following day and I waited outside the Manager's Office for the Auckland Blues, for whom Eden Park is their home ground. It was Sunday morning and the manager came in to do some paperwork – none other than Graham Henry.

The hearing was a clear cut affair and Venter and I were asked to leave the room while the committee deliberated. We sat in Graham Henry's office and began to chat. He told me he'd gone for the ball and missed it, but he didn't deny that he'd caught Fitzpatrick's head. Venter is an engineer so we had something in common. We spoke about things other than rugby and although I have no sentiment for anyone committing foul play I thought he was a nice guy. It was obvious that the incident was out of character for him, a proverbial moment of madness. While we waited for the verdict one of the disciplinary panel put his head around the door and shouted down the corridor for a calendar. Venter's face dropped. If the panel needed a calendar the suspension must be a long one. In the event he received a fine and a three week ban. He reckoned his wife would be the only happy person because she would see more of him for a while. There was a post-script to the incident the following year when South Africa toured France and I was selected to referee the test in Lyon. It was another super game of rugby, which France just edged. Venter played in the game and at the after-match function he came over and asked me to autograph the red card for him to take home for his club. We shook hands and had our photograph taken with me giving him the red card for a second time! I've always followed his performances since then.

If It Wasn't for the Players...

Referees get what they deserve from players, so if you let one man rabbit on and on, others will soon join in. I always asked them once to stop talking, let them carry on until play was at a kickable position, then threw in the penalty. It costs them points, the captain wants to know about it and so you solve the problem. I don't know why the hookers are always the ones doing the talking. Perhaps it's because you're always there with them. I can walk into a clubhouse after a game and I always know who the front row players are but if a winger comes up to you afterwards you don't recognize them, unless they're seasoned internationals.

I remember an English hooker called Steve Brain. I was on the touch at Twickenham for England vs Ireland in the snow. It was March 1st – St David's Day – in 1986. Clive Norling was the referee and Ken Rowlands was on the other touch. In those days, if there was foul play the touch judge had to stick out his flag towards the offending side. Ciaran Fitzgerald was the Irish captain and hooker. It was a period when England didn't have a very good side. England won the ball at a maul, threw it wide and one of their backs dived over for a try in the corner. But I'd spotted Brain punching Fitzgerald at the maul. Clive was awarding the try and Ken was running behind the posts for the conversion. But I stood my ground on the touchline and held my flag out. Because the crowd could see it was pointing towards England, you can imagine the response. Ken started looking around for me and saw that I was back on the ten metre line. Clive came over and I told him what I'd seen. He asked me for a decision. I told him that the try should be disallowed and a penalty should be awarded to Ireland. And that's what happened. The crowd were booing and whistling and they started throwing snowballs at me. The cameramen along the touchline had been annoying me all afternoon but they were being hit as well. England held on to win by 25-20.

Everybody in the northern hemisphere thinks that All Blacks captain and hooker Sean Fitzpatrick tried to referee the game. He would, *if* you let him but I had no problems with him at all. When he talked to the referee it was almost as if he was trying to help, if that doesn't sound too strange. I enjoyed refereeing him and I enjoyed his company off the field. He's got a tremendous amount to offer the game. Everyone thinks that when he was seen talking all the time that he was getting at the referee but that's not the case. Very often he was just goading the opposition. I always found him an excellent captain to communicate with, as I did with South Africa's Francois Pienaar. They were men who were obviously in charge of their teams. Of course, referees should penalise captains or march them back ten metres like any other player. Just because they're the captain doesn't give them the right to mouth off to the referee. But, pre-match, I would always ask the captain to talk to me during the game if he had a problem and I would try to sort it out. I wouldn't have to agree with them but at least we would be communicating.

Wayne Shelford was an excellent captain and there weren't any problems with him. The Whetton brothers, Garry and Alan were great as well. On the other hand Phil Kearns didn't seem to be a popular Australian captain and he would talk down to referees. Nick Farr-Jones was the best Australian captain I dealt with. He was very talkative but a very intelligent rugby player who could read a game. Not many players have picked up the World Cup, but he's done it. Michael Lynagh is a real gent both on and off the field: a real class act. David Campese was a bit aloof but we had some banter between us. He would say "I don't agree with that!" and I would reply "I don't care what you agree with!" On another occasion he came out with "Just because you're the referee doesn't make you right all the time." My reply to that was "Just because you're an international winger doesn't mean you know the laws!" You don't change your style at all when you're refereeing southern hemisphere sides and I don't believe there's a lot of difference with their referees either. In Australia for example, rugby union is way behind other sports in popularity so during the late 1980s the ARU encouraged their referees to make the game attractive to pull in the spectators. Crowds didn't pay to hear the referees whistle so they've been more laid back. If there was an opportunity not to blow the whistle then they wouldn't. But now the IRB appoints all test match referees so everyone must toe the line.

South Africa were to play the final match of their tour to France and the UK against the Barbarians in Dublin and I had been appointed for this match. Earlier in the tour I was number four when South Africa played Neath in the now infamous 'Battle of the Gnoll'. It was a ferocious game with two major stand-up fights. You couldn't take your eyes off it. The officials were all from Scotland and the referee was Ray Megson, a barrister from Edinburgh. From my viewpoint on the side of the pitch I thought that the problems in the game stemmed from the South African hooker, James Dalton, who continuously goaded the Neath players. Megson didn't sort him out and this led to all the niggle during the game. After the final whistle Megson didn't agree with me and said Dalton gave him no problems. But I made a mental note that if I came across Dalton I would have to deal with him at the beginning of the game.

Naturally Dalton was selected as hooker for South Africa against the Barbarians at Lansdowne Road. The Barbarians committee had been wise and selected many Irishmen in their line up including the complete front row of Clohessy, Wood and Popplewell. Wales's Robert Jones was the captain. The game began and at the first line-out, Dalton started to rabbit – "Come on ref, are we playing offside or what?" The first scrum came a few minutes later and he hadn't stopped talking. Both sets of packs were in the crouch position and the front rows were ready to get stuck in. This was my opportunity. "Stop there" I said. "Green hooker. I don't know what you've been used to but I'm not going to put up with your talking all through the game. You're not the captain so SHUT UP." Then a wonderful Irish voice was heard from the Barbarians front row. "Would you like us to shut him up for you Mr Bevan?" I declined the invitation with a big smile on my face. The Barbarians won the game, 23-15.

Brian 'The Pit Bull' Moore, the England hooker, was another

character. He seemed to have a wonderful gift for rubbing his opponents the wrong way. And he played on the edge. His offside lines and his jabbering would push you, as a referee, to your limits. I really disliked players chopsing to me during a game, it disrupted my concentration, which is no doubt why they did it. I had to apply my one warning followed by a penalty in a kickable position strategy several times with Brian. But off the field, Brian is a very likeable chap. I had the pleasure of his company on a Barbarians trip to Zurich, to promote the game in Switzerland. They loved him there. He plays the guitar, sings and joins in the fun. But on the field he had a job to do, and if he could gain any sort of advantage against his opponent or the referee, he'd do his best to get it.

Rugby can provoke some funny stories off the field too. At Twickenham in 1992, England scored a try in the first minute of the game against Ireland through their full back Jonathan Webb. He is a doctor and after the game he told me that he whilst he was doing a ward visit at the hospital where he worked he looked in on a young boy he had been treating. The boy's father was there and he told Jon how much he admired him as a player for England. The boy said "But Dad, you said he was crap!"

I've been caught out a couple of times myself. In 1982, during one of my earlier first class matches I was in the middle for an Anglo-Welsh friendly between Newbridge and Saracens. There was a maul near the Saracens' line. One of the Newbridge forwards emerged from it and dived over the line. I blew for the try. Then one of the Saracens' players asked what my decision was, and I confirmed that I'd awarded the try for Newbridge. "But shouldn't he have this?" he asked, and held up the ball. The Newbridge forward had dived over empty handed and I'd been conned. It was all done in fun and I changed my decision to scrum five, Saracens ball!

In 1987 I was refereeing a club match at the Arms Park between Cardiff and Llanelli. The roof of the stand there, underneath the old National Stadium, protruded quite far towards the touch line. The ball was kicked to touch and the linesman put up his flag, but the ball then veered in-field, so it was play on. This happened more than once. The game was hotting up and I had to keep a close eye on any off-the-ball incidents. Gerald Cordle, the Cardiff wing, kicked ahead and, instead of watching the flight of the ball I kept my eye on Cordle to make sure I didn't miss any late tackle. Everything was okay so I looked for the ball, which was in-field. The touch judge had his flag up but I waved play on. The players were dumbfounded: I hadn't seen that the ball had hit the roof of the stand and then come back on to the field. It should have been a lineout but I was the only person in the ground who didn't know.

I had an embarrassing moment in front of the television cameras at the end of January 1998 at Ebbw Vale when Pontypridd were the visitors. It was a Saturday evening match and the following Saturday I was due to referee France against England in the first match at the new Stade de France. France and England are mean matches, there's no love lost in these fixtures and I was really looking forward to the encounter. I was enjoying the match at Ebbw Vale but I got too close to the play and was caught up in a tackle which took my legs from underneath me. I fell awkwardly. My brother Wyn was watching the game in the Vardre Club. Vardre had had a home game so the clubhouse was packed. When I went down somebody shouted out "The ginger bastard is down!" I was in agony and as I lay on the floor with my ankle swollen, one of the players came over and asked me "Whose ball is it, ref?" I had to be carried off the field and as I lay down in the dressing room my assessor came in to tell me how many penalties I'd given! My thoughts turned to the international the following week and I knew I wouldn't make it. I was given until the Tuesday to recover but I wasn't close to it, indeed I was out of action for a month.

Other Tours and Tournaments

One of the benefits of being an international referee is the international travel: five star hotels, top class cuisine, trips to the sights... I've seen the world, though not all of it was as high-flying as the previous sentence suggests. A few chapters back I described my first tour, a fun trip to Japan with Ireland, but there have been more trying times, often when I've refereed in the emerging rugby nations. I participated in a four-way tournament in Moscow in 1989, between Russia, Romania, Poland and Crawshay's Welsh. The teams all played each other so there was practically a game every day. We stayed in a hotel which was five star rated by Russian standards but closer to minus two by ours. It was a dreadful place just off Red Square. From the window of my room I could see military guards and the famous buildings surrounding Red Square.

Most of the people we met were very poor, and the shops were bare. I suppose I shouldn't complain, but the food in the hotel was dreadful. What there was of it was barely edible. The hotel staff pilfered anything they could. One evening we we saw a waitress steal a large piece of cheese from the kitchen. Later we were told that cheese was off the menu that night. The players marked their bread rolls and the same ones turned up for breakfast, lunch and dinner for three days! The bar opened for two hours every evening and sold only vodka. It was vodka and orange, vodka and lime, and nothing else. A large Russian lady sat at a desk on each floor to oversee the rooms. The bathrooms were full of beetles; there was no soap, toilet paper or shampoo and the towels were only fit to wash cars.

Nevertheless, we were there to play rugby. The stadium, in the Moscow suburbs, was archaic and not very well equipped. The first game was Russia vs Romania. There was no admission charge because there wouldn't have been any spectators. Even with free admission only about six hundred people turned out to watch. After the game both teams and the officials shared the showers in a very long, rather prison-like room. The suds from my shampoo drifted down a channel in the middle of the shower room and I became aware that everyone was looking at me. It was such a rare event for someone to have shampoo that they wanted to see who it was. I was the only one in over thirty men who had soap and shampoo.

The normal practice after a game in a foreign country or when overseas referees visit is to exchange pin badges, or even ties. But the Russian and the Romanian who had been my touch judges only wanted my soap, shampoo and aftershave. Everyone wanted to exchange money with you so they could obtain hard currency. Local people stopped us in the street and offered to buy our track-suits and training shoes. Soldiers stationed outside the hotel (because it was for tourists) offered to sell their uniforms, even their guns. One of the Crawshay's players bought a uniform to use in fancy dress parties back in Wales.

I tried to buy some fruit but couldn't find a greengrocers. While I was sightseeing one morning a lorry pulled up on a street corner and unloaded sacks of potatoes onto the kerbside. The driver brought out weighing scales and a seat, and a queue formed immediately. As we walked around we were easily spotted as tourists. If you put out your hand for a taxi an ordinary, private car stopped and offered to take you anywhere for hard currency and half the price of an official taxi. You had to jump in quickly before the official taxi turned up or the private taxi would be in trouble. There was a lot of risk involved for the person doing it but the extra money made it worthwhile. When I joined the Crawshay's team for a bus trip into the country outside Moscow I couldn't believe the way the people lived. What I'd assumed were cowsheds were actually houses, houses with just cardboard on the windows to keep out the cold winters. Back in Moscow early one evening we heard gunfire outside the hotel. There had been a robbery. The culprit ignored police orders to stop so they shot him outside the door of the hotel.

There was top quality hospitality, too. The Crawshay's Committee, Keith Rowlands of the IRB and I were invited to dinner by the Georgia Rugby Union. Georgia is a rich, agricultural land which wanted to join the IRB. After the awful hotel food we accepted the invitation eagerly and looked forward to the occasion. The dinner was held in the hotel, but in a private function room on the top floor which could be reached only in a special lift – the normal ones stopped at the floor below. We had caviar, Georgian wine and one of the finest cognacs I've ever tasted, with rich dark black coffee. It would have been a beautiful meal under normal conditions but after four days of hotel fare it was a sumptuous feast. At the other end of the scale we had a great evening at the British Embassy. They had McEwan's lager and Newcastle Brown Ale, crisps and nuts! We hadn't seen crisps and nuts for a week! The tournament itself was something of a non-event and rather incidental. The standard wasn't great. The Russian side included a number of policemen and the Russian referees were afraid to referee them too strictly: I ended up refereeing every game involving Russia. The Romanians played some attractive rugby but the tournament was won by Crawshay's, who had Rupert Moon, Brian Williams, Glyn Llewellyn, Hemi Taylor and Glen Webbe in their side.

Dubai, one of the United Arab Emirates, was a complete contrast to Russia. It was already a wealthy country after centuries of trading, but now through oil wealth it has developed as a holiday destination and sporting capital of the Middle East. The hotels are second to none and the palaces of the Sheiks are as big as villages – no expense is spared on them. The visible wealth is almost obscene. The police drive Mercedes and there's no crime. At the hotel beach clubs you can quite happily leave your wallet and money on the table next to your sun lounger whilst you swim in the sea without a worry that anything will be stolen. An International Sevens tournament is held there every year at the Dubai Exiles Club in conjunction with a Gulf tournament. The local teams consist mostly of ex-pats and when I visited there in 1994 all the matches were played on sand pitches. The sand is compacted by rollers but cuts up quite badly and the Club now has a couple of grass pitches for World Cup events. During an interview with Owen Jenkins, who was there for Welsh television, he asked me what it was like to referee on sand. I replied that I didn't have any problems because I used rubbers. I realised what I'd said immediately and we had to stop the interview because we'd both collapsed in fits of laughter.

The temperature can be in the nineties even in November when the Sevens are held. It's a great tournament: the welcome is great and the organisation superb. There is a big party atmosphere but the rugby in the international competition is very serious indeed. Some of the biggest names, like Michael Lynagh and Jonah Lomu, have played there. The Dubai Exiles Club was like a home from home for me because there ware so many Welshmen involved there – inevitably, they're known as The Taffia.

Another great sevens event is the Heineken Tournament in Amsterdam. There was no danger of a pitch with a slope there! It's been hit by the professionalisation of the British game though. Clubs are much less willing to allow highly paid players to take part. What began as a fun tournament and developed into something much more competitive has found itself shorn of some of the top, crowd-drawing teams. It's a shame, I've refereed there about eight times over a period of nearly twenty years and it's a good tournament.

But the greatest sevens tournament is undoubtedly the Hong Kong Sevens. I was invited there in 1988. The crowd was incredible – it's a real party atmosphere. But for some reason – I don't know why – they had taken against Australia that year. Anyone who played the Wallabies was guaranteed fantastic support. As the Aussies walked past the main grandstand to warm up before their matches they were whistled and booed while their opponents were cheered. In one of the pool matches, I refereed Australia against Taiwan. Of course, the Aussies were winning easily but all their tries were greeted by the crowd with howls of derision. During a rare attack by Taiwan an Australian player knocked on the ball near his line. It wasn't deliberate but I thought this was an opportunity to be loved by the crowd, so I ran beneath the posts and awarded a penalty try. I was given a standing ovation – the crowd went mad. David Campese realised what had happened: "You know how to milk it, don't you?" he said. But the Australians took it in good spirit, fair play to them. I was honoured to be awarded the final between New Zealand and France. 'Buck' Shelford was captain of New Zealand and Laurent Rodriguez captained France: two international number eight forwards. It was an amazing sight to see these two go at each other in a three-man scrum. They didn't budge an inch. It was a tough game, with fierce tackling, which New Zealand won.

One of the nicest countries I've visited is Zimbabwe. I went there in 1982 with Swansea, and in addition to the rugby visited Victoria Falls and went on safari. I enjoyed the climate and I found the people very kind. I was invited to referee a schoolboy game on a Saturday morning, and as we approached the ground there were cars everywhere. I thought it must be market day but it turned out that the match was between the top two public schools in Zimbabwe. As I walked into the ground all the kids doffed their hats to me – not a things referees are used to! It was a big event with marquees everywhere and a crowd of around three and a half thousand.

That was a special occasion with well-appointed facilities. The most unusual pitch I've refereed on was in Munich, in 1987 during the Oktoberfest – the huge beer festival. It's a slightly bigger affair than Clydach carnival. There was a tournament which included teams from the British Armed Forces in Germany. The best pitch they could muster was a soccer pitch with two uprights lashed either side to protrude above the crossbar. The soccer nets were still in place so if anyone scored underneath the posts they had to be careful not to get tangled up. Most of the lines were the soccer ones, too. Thankfully it was a sevens tournament so it didn't matter too much. In fact it was quite a good competition with Army teams up against ones from the RAF, so things got quite fierce. Added to that was the fun of the Oktoberfest with drinking sheds up to six hundred yards long and Bavarian music playing all day. It was a great atmosphere but hardly cultural!

Referees and the WRU

Over the years I've had three Chairmen of Referees at the WRU. The first one was the late Rod Morgan, who I found supportive and who told me he liked my style of refereeing. However there was one incident, early in my career, when he frightened me. He was a high-ranking police officer and had a reputation as a hard but fair man. I was refereeing Swansea against Neath at St Helen's. It was a strong Neath pack which didn't lie down for anyone. It was a pat on the back for me to be appointed to this fixture and signified that I was on the way up. The TV cameras were there but play seemed to be stuck down in the bottom corner near the grandstand at the Mumbles end and we had a succession of scrum fives. It was a typically tough game between these two rivals. Barry Clegg had left Swansea to play for Neath, and he and Dick Moriarty were having a good old tussle. We were close to the crowd and I could hear one Neath supporter shouting at me all the time. He was calling me all the names under the sun – most of them unprintable.

We couldn't seem to get away from this part of the field. Then a Neath player was injured and there were accusations of foul play. This made the supporter more angry and again he kept on at me. I'm ashamed to admit it, but I lost my cool and I gave him a two-fingered salute. In those days there were no neutral touch judges, the lines were run by a committeeman from each club, so the referee couldn't rely on any help from them. I was on my own in the dressing room after the game – the touch judges were with their own teams. Rod came down from the stand and his face was quite mellow. "It was a very tough game," he said "well done, well controlled." I thanked him, feeling good about myself. But then his face turned to thunder and he pointed his finger straight at me and said "If you ever do that again, I'll make sure that you'll never referee another game in Wales!" The colour drained from my face and I asked him what he meant. He came back at me: "You know exactly what I mean. If you can't take stick out in the middle from the people on the terrace then get out of it now! If you as a referee stick two fingers up at a supporter then the next thing he's over the fence and we could have an assault. Then the police have to take action which means rugby gets like soccer and we have to put fences around the grounds, just because people like you cannot take abuse. Don't you ever do that again!" Then he turned and walked out of the room. I went from a feeling of elation to hating myself in a matter of moments. It was another lesson learned.

Rod was succeeded by Denzil Lloyd, who was an international referee himself. Denzil was a big fan of Clive Norling but gradually he came around and supported us equally. In the past he had been involved with us as an assessor. I've always remembered the advice he gave me not to change my style and I've now passed this on to young referees on their way up the ladder. Denzil was also very honest. After I'd had a torrid time in a game between Llanelli against Pontypridd, when I was having a poor period, I wasn't given an appointment in the Five Nations. It was during the period when the Rugby Unions still appointed their own officials to nominated fixtures. Clive and Les were given matches but I wasn't. I asked Denzil whether the appointments were significant to form and he said "Absolutely". And that was as it should be. He told me that I wasn't refereeing at my best and he was absolutely correct.

Terry Vaux was the third Chairman of Referees in my time and he was also very supportive. I asked him to 'give me the nod' when the time came, so that if I wasn't refereeing well I could retire before I was dropped. When I did decide to retire he said that he hadn't forgotten what I had told him, but that it hadn't been necessary. Terry is a Gwent man but despite that he didn't favour Les, another Gwent man, above anyone else.

During my refereeing career, the WRU decided to appoint a full-time Referees' Development Officer. The first person to hold this post was Ken Rowlands from Ynysybwl. An ex-international referee, he is a man of immense knowledge. When he spoke about the art of refereeing, most people listened. As time went on, we became very good friends and I'm sure that he helped me achieve many of my ambitions. He could be moody, especially on a Monday morning when all the complaints were coming in about weekend refereeing performances, but he would support a referee if he thought the criticism was unfair. He was terrific during the 1991 World Cup and it's a great shame that he was unable to be there in 1999. Unfortunately, at that time his lovely wife Kath was not well and it was impossible for him to carry on full-time employment. It was sad, because he was so popular around the world. He was a character who loved to enjoy himself, like me! I remember Denzil Lloyd saying to us both, that it was a good thing that we weren't too long on the Panel together, otherwise we could have been quite a dangerous partnership!

Ken was replaced by Clive Norling, who is a totally different type of person. It's widely felt that Clive wants to be the centre of attention. He'd be the first to admit that, although his style of refereeing would suit the modern game, it wouldn't be in tune with the modern administrators. They want technical infringements punished whereas Clive's strength was to keep the game flowing. As Director of Referees at the WRU he's something of a poacher turned gamekeeper. I didn't feel that I had the same support from Clive, that Ken gave me. But every man has his own methods of doing things and perhaps Clive was looking ahead and concentrated on the young, future international referees.

The Welsh Society of Rugby Union Referees is divided into nine Districts. In the past it lacked a strong voice and accepted what it was given, which wasn't very much. In the early days of my career we had to supply our own kit, even our own whistle! But the system which now exists for referees is excellent. The Welsh referee is well looked after, with free kit, physiotherapy and good match fees and expenses. This is the result of referees fighting hard for an adequate deal, and some common sense from the WRU. The Society's Secretary is Hugh Banfield, from Loughor, a strong-willed, very intelligent man and a good referee. He's not afraid to speak his mind or to put forward the feelings of the Society. And, of course, he doesn't go ahead with anything without the majority vote of the nine District Societies.

I take my hat off to him. He was a key figure for the referees when we had a major point of conflict with the WRU. As the game became professional we, as referees, believed we should have a match fee, in line with other countries. We approached the WRU with our ideas but were turned down. However, we remained firm and the Society decided that referees should withdraw their labour for one Saturday – 21 December 1996 – in other words, a strike. I was due to referee Cardiff against Swansea that day but I was determined not to be there. The WRU were informed that the strike could be called off at very short notice, by just one phone call. I couldn't understand that the WRU hadn't seen this coming: we really meant business. Only half a dozen or so matches were played that Saturday, mostly in the lower divisions. I spent the afternoon watching my twin sons play soccer.

I was saddened that the whole affair had been allowed to go so far. The strike was simultaneously necessary and unnecessary. It was necessary for the referees to stand up and make their case, but unnecessary because the WRU could have done something about it. Did they really think the issue would just go away? It would have been better for the game if they had addressed it before the strike. We didn't feel victorious when the WRU immediately began negotiating with us on the terms of a match fee. There would be a sliding scale of fees from £200 for the top graded games down to £40 for Division 3, plus mileage expenses. Once things moved, they moved quickly. The referees realised that they had a considerable amount of power, that matches couldn't go ahead without us. But it isn't an influence we wanted to abuse.

An Indulgence

During my career I've had the pleasure of refereeing some of the great names in world rugby. I don't expect everyone to agree with the following selections, but in Wales two people can't select the same side anyway. This is my personal choice of those I have been in the middle with:

Welsh XV

15. J.P.R. Williams
Everything has been said about him, he was world class.
14. Ieuan Evans
A great finisher.
13. Ray Gravell
Hard, strong, competitive and a great talker!
12. Steve Fenwick
Always creating opportunities for his fellow players.
11. J.J. Williams
A player who could score tries from impossible situations.
10. Phil Bennett
Only he could follow the great Barry John.
9. Terry Holmes
Just had the edge over David Bishop who I thought was an outstanding competitor. Sadly I never refereed Gareth Edwards in a competitive game.
1. Charlie Faulkner 2. Bobby Windsor 3. Graham Price
The Pontypool front row as a trio worked so well together. As individuals they just didn't look the same.

4. Geoff Wheel
Hard worker with terrific upper body strength.
5. Robert Norster
World class second row who could win the ball without being lifted.
6. Dai Morris
Everybody's favourite.
7. Terry Cobner
Captain – a great leader.
8. Jeff Squire
Had great vision for the game.

J.P.R. and Norster would get into a World XV but these are players for a Rest of the World XV:

15. Serge Blanco (France)
Exciting and you never knew what he would do next.
14. David Campese (Australia)
Wonderfully arrogant.
13. Phillippe Sella (France)
Always seemed to do the correct things.
12. Tim Horan (Australia)
Definitely not a soft centre.
11. Jonah Lomu (New Zealand)
Have you ever tried to stop a tank - ask the Underwoods!
10. Michael Lynagh (Australia)
A perfect gentleman and an outstanding all round player.
9. Nick Farr-Jones (Australia)
Captain – Always in the right place at the right time.
1. Steve McDowell (New Zealand)
Solid as a rock and good in the loose.
2. Keith Wood (Ireland)
I think he's a fabulous player.
3. Os du Rant (South Africa)
Very powerful.
4. John Eales (Australia)
Modest, talented and has deserved his many successes.
5. Mark Andrews (South Africa)
A hard worker with great ball skills for a big man.

6. Michael Jones (New Zealand)
Immense supporter of the ball carrier.
7. Lawrence Dallaglio (England)
A complete back row player.
8. Zinzan Brooke (New Zealand)
Brought back row play to a new dimension.

My Final Season

I had decided that my final season would be that of the 1999 Rugby World Cup. I knew that there was no chance of my being around for the 2003 World Cup so I wanted to go out at the top of my career. The last thing I wanted to hear people say was, 'I remember Derek Bevan when he was a good referee'. There was a point at the beginning of the season when I contemplated retiring right after the World Cup. But Clive Norling persuaded me to stay on and finish the season. In agreeing to that I stressed to Clive that I would be looking for a full season and that I should be considered for everything. I didn't just want to make up the numbers. No promises were given to me and equally I didn't ask for or expect any in return.

After the World Cup the international appointments were announced for the Six Nations, Tri-Nations and the tour matches. I was appointed to run touch for England vs Ireland and my final international match as referee was to be Ireland against Italy in Dublin. Although it may not have been the biggest fixture at least I would be refereeing my first and last Home International match at my favourite ground. I couldn't think of a better place to finish my international career than Lansdowne Road and it was also a wonderful opportunity to be involved with the Italians in their first Six Nations. So I was quite happy.

But before I could think too much about that it was straight in to the domestic season in Wales and the European Cup and Conference. League matches in Wales had continued during the period of the World Cup. Again I was involved in matches in France, Italy and England. Because I had already made my decision to retire

I was completely relaxed. I had never contemplated retiring before. Some referees have decided to pack it in earlier because they'd become disillusioned or had some poor performances, but it hadn't crossed my mind. I've had my fair share of criticism and poor matches but it hadn't made me think of hanging up my boots. However, this was to be the end.

The season was one of 'the last time in....'. When I was in Italy my thoughts turned to the fact that it would be my last visit to these grounds. I refereed London Irish against Brive at the Stoop and knew it would be my last time there. I've been to Toulouse about six times and it was like meeting old friends. They told me I should carry on but you have to draw the line somewhere. The fitness element was getting harder. We went through the funny side of it at the beginning of RWC 1999 but it was getting more difficult as the standards were raised, and I do enjoy my social life! I still help out with social and fun tournaments, and my beloved Cwmtawe Sevens. Common sense is now telling me that I have made the correct decision.

My mother, Doreen, is thrilled that I've retired. If she knew I was refereeing and the game was on television, she wouldn't watch until she'd found out afterwards that everything had gone okay. Then she'd watch a tape of the game! She wouldn't watch it live in case something went wrong or the commentator said something derogatory about me! She's changed her papers so many times. She would buy the *Western Mail* until a reporter criticized my refereeing. Then she'd stop buying that paper and turn to another one, and so on. She would even stop buying a paper if there was criticism of me in a reader's letter! So she can choose any paper she wants to from now on.

It was a trouble-free season. After so many years on the circuit I'd got to the point where my reputation preceded me. I was given respect by the players. But this is a good lesson to young referees, you must earn respect. When it became common knowledge that I was to retire Clive told me that he'd never had so many requests for a particular referee. He said he could only put me in one place on a Saturday! I did the West Wales final at Stradey between Llandovery and Dunvant. When it was announced at the Gnoll in Neath that it was my last game there, the crowd gave a huge cheer! But to be fair to them they also gave me a standing ovation. I've been booed off the park there on more than one occasion so I was quite choked, and the club presented me with some cut glass after the game. The generosity of the clubs was overwhelming, not only at the big clubs but also smaller ones like Cwmllynfell. Perhaps they were all glad to see the back of me!

My refereeing was very relaxed. I didn't have to worry about assessors any more. After one or two assessments immediately following the World Cup, Clive realized it was a waste of time. Although you're never too old to learn there wasn't much point in them in my last season. Even the coaches must have thought there wasn't any use having a go at me since I wouldn't be around for much longer – not that I ever listened to coaches anyway. One of my strengths was appearing to listen to coaches and then forgetting everything they told me.

My final international, at Lansdowne Road, was tinged with sadness. I might have hinted to Steve Griffiths of the IRB during the World Cup that it would be wonderful to end my international career in Dublin! Everyone there is marvellous. Even the Ireland coach Warren Gatland, who is a Kiwi, has fallen in to the Irish way of life. He even talks like an Irishman now. Syd Millar always puts me in a headlock when I get there and says "How are you, you Welsh bastard?" People don't do that anywhere else, and certainly not at Twickenham. Even the physio offers me some liniment.

I couldn't relax my preparations for this particular game. I was still a professional being paid a fee to referee an international game. The last thing I wanted in my final international was to be remembered for a poor performance. My touch judges were Stuart Dickinson from Australia and Brian Campsall of England – both terrific company. The evening before we went around the corner from the hotel and had a quiet Italian meal. Unusually, I slept well that night. Normally before an international I would toss and turn all night. It's difficult not to think about the following day's game, though I never carried a law book with me – it spoils a good game! Common sense needs to prevail. In Referees Society meetings, the others would laugh when I was asked some specific questions about the laws of the game.

Ireland vs Italy didn't need a lot of refereeing because it was so one-sided. I told both captains before the kick off that I didn't want to issue any yellow or red cards in my last international. I said that I was in the mood for a good open game. Keith Wood, the Irish hooker and captain agreed with me. The Italian captain said nothing. Ireland hit Italy in the first half and the game was over by the interval. The Italians came back at Irish in the second half but had too much ground to make up. I just let the game go and turned a blind eye to minor infringements. We had some fake injuries towards the end because the game was so fast. Ireland won 60-13, but I didn't realize at the final whistle that it was the end for me. It only sank in later. Woody presented me with an Irish jersey and the Italians gave me an Azure one. I received ties, cuff links and a pen set.

The flight back to Cardiff was a lonely one. My Italian is non-existent and I've never felt the need to learn any phrases of French either. English is such a common language that most teams understand what they need to. When you're penalizing the French they don't seem to know any English but when you're having a conversation with them in the bar afterwards, they seem to understand it well enough. I remember a 'B' international in Lyon in my early days and Camberabero was captain of the French against Scotland. On the field he couldn't speak a word of English but his after-match speech was superb, spoken in perfect English. I came across him ten years later in a European fixture between Ulster and Begles-Bordeaux and he was, once again, the captain. When we tossed up, I asked him "English?" "Non," he replied, "just a little." I reminded him of that match in Lyon and his speech afterwards: "But it is improving all the time," he said. I certainly miss the European dimension. My final match in Europe as referee was Toulouse against Padova. Another nice place to finish as I have many friends down there.

Back in Wales I soon knew that I wouldn't get the Welsh Challenge Cup Final. Clive informed the referees involved at the quarter final stages. Clayton and I were to have the semifinals, both to be played in the Millennium Stadium on the same day. Nigel Whitehouse was the man for the final itself. At this point I hadn't refereed at the Millennium Stadium. The opportunity hadn't arisen during the World Cup, and I desperately wanted to do so before the end of my career. Obviously, I wanted to be part of the final because I had officiated at sixteen consecutive finals, including four as referee. Clive and I jointly hold the record of four finals. But there's no sentiment in rugby and I couldn't expect to be given the final just because it was my last year. There were members of the Welsh Rugby Union who had told me that they felt that I should have refereed the 2000 Final. Clive's job is to appoint and he doesn't have to give any reasons. I can't believe there was anything vindictive in his decision not to appoint me for the Final.

My semifinal was Llanelli vs Ebbw Vale, the first to be played that day. Ebbw Vale seemed to be overcome by the occasion. Llanelli are the cup kings and had been to this stage so many times before. It was a thrilling experience to be given the match there though it was a disappointing crowd and the stadium was far from being full. The match was notable for one of the quickest tries in any game. The ball was kicked off, the Ebbw Vale forwards caught it, it was passed back to the outside half who kicked for touch. The ball was charged down and Wayne Proctor scored for Llanelli in a matter of seconds. Llanelli built up a lead and although Ebbw Vale came back at them in the last quarter Llanelli were too far in front.

My last match in the League was a mid-week fixture: Cardiff against an under-strength Llanelli side who had qualified for the European Cup semifinal. Llanelli still played exceptionally well and it was a close affair which Cardiff won. As the time came to blow the whistle I played about four minutes of injury time and genuinely thought that it was my last game. It just seemed like the end of another hard season of rugby. I received a club plaque from Cardiff and a jersey, and an invitation to their annual dinner. The following day I discovered that it wasn't my last game. Clive informed me that I was to referee Wales against the French Barbarians.

Everybody said that this additional game was going to be fun but I've always been suspicious about matches involving the French Barbarians. One of the finest games of rugby I ever refereed was their centenary against England at Twickenham in 1991. Although it wasn't a first choice French team for the game against Wales there were some notorious names in their line-up. I had refereed Wales once previously when John Ryan was the Welsh coach and he decided to play warm up matches against two Welsh club sides. I did them against Bridgend, when Wales lost! Although I knew the French Barbarians was to be my very last game I couldn't take anything for granted. My touch judges were Clayton and Nigel Whitehouse and I told them that we would have to take it as the players wanted to play it. I didn't want to finish on a low. I did a TV interview with Ray Gravell before the kick off and there was quite a lot of coverage for me in the media during the week. There was a little bit of disappointment that there wasn't a full house.

The game was tough and hard: we even had a fist being thrown and threats of a yellow card from myself to one of the Frenchmen. There was some nice rugby and good traditional stuff. Towards the end of the game both Clayton and Nigel kept reminding me, "Not long to go now Bev", and I knew that this really would be IT. I dragged things out as long as I could and I added on about four minutes, which was quite enough because the French were getting too close to Wales! I looked at my watch and I could see the cameras were on me so I gave the whistle one long, last blast.

The crowd all stood and the players stayed on the field. Skrella, the French coach came over as did Jacques Fouroux who said "Finit"? All the French came over and shook my hand. The players did a lap of honour and Nigel urged me to do the same but I couldn't do it. I just waved to the crowd and did a lot of handshaking. There were no tears and the crowd was fantastic. Graham Henry wished me luck. Mark Taylor, the Welsh captain for the day presented me with a Welsh jersey, which meant a lot to me. I received a tie from the French Barbarians which was a great honour because you have to play for them to get one. It was a very special day, probably more special for myself than any of the players. I woke up the following day to a headache and the newspapers, which were very kind. My mother was happy and she's kept all the articles!

When I decided to retire I never imagined that my final season after a twenty-eight year career would be overshadowed by events off the field. Three things happened to me which have had a major effect on my life. I was burgled, I was awarded the MBE and I became a grandfather.

I was renting a house while I waited to buy a property. A lot of my belongings were sitting in boxes but I had unpacked some treasured mementoes, acquired over the years, so that I would have some familiar things about the house. The burglars forced their way in through the kitchen window. I was fast asleep upstairs and the only sound I heard was the front door slamming as they made off. They even stole my car, the keys had been on the kitchen table. They had stolen electrical appliances like the TV and video, which could easily be replaced, but they also stole a lot of the souvenirs and jerseys which I had collected over the years. They took a beautiful Waterford Crystal ball which had been presented to me by the Irish Rugby Union, fine brandy goblets and a brandy decanter on a wooden stand presented by the Welsh Referees' Society for refereeing the 1991 World Cup Final. Irreplaceable. They also stole a replica of the Millennium Stadium which Sir Tasker Watkins had presented to me. In my new home I have a photograph of Sir Tasker presenting me with something I haven't got anymore!

The police believe that the thieves were stealing in the dark and when they saw that what they had taken couldn't be sold on they probably dumped it in the canal. My car was found some weeks later with £2,000 worth of damage to it. I couldn't sleep at all after the burglary and I went to bed with a hammer next to me. But even during this low period there was a great deal of humour. After I refereed the West Wales Final between Dunvant and Llandovery I was presented with a shield for my retirement. Dai Vaughan of Dunvant said that because of the burglary I now had plenty of room on the shelf to display it! I replied that the only thing that the burglars left behind was my Dunvant tie!

Towards the end of my last season, I had accepted an invitation to referee an RAF tens tournament in Cyprus. I had a great time – no pressure at all and a pint of lager in the Officers' Mess was forty-eight pence, a scotch was twenty-seven pence and only fifty pence for a double. Needless to say we didn't move far from the Mess! I had phoned home from Cyprus and I had been told that my daughter Alison, who was pregnant wasn't very well so when I arrived back I was eager to discover how she was. My mother asked me "Do you know you're a grandfather?" I thought she was pulling my leg because this was fourteen and a half weeks before the baby was due to be born. I went immediately from the airport to Singleton Hospital's Baby Care Unit in Swansea. Alison looked awful, she'd obviously been through a lot. We went to see the baby who'd been named Samuel and who was in an incubator. He was only two pounds and two ounces when he was born – the weight of a bag of sugar. He was wrapped in a blanket: there were tubes everywhere and he was being fed by a tube through his nose. I cried with Alison. I went home that night and I did something that I hadn't done in a long time. I prayed. I didn't want it for myself, I wanted it for Alison and little Samuel. Someone must have been listening to me because eight weeks later Sam came out of the incubator and was developing well. Although I was a chapel-goer when I was younger and I wouldn't describe myself as being deeply religious, this has had a tremendous affect on me. My prayers had been answered so there must be something which I can't explain. But then, there must be others who've also prayed in similar circumstances but things didn't work out for them. But for me, there is a God there and he does listen even if you're not a regular. The late Kerry Fitzgerald always prayed before a game. He didn't ask us as touch judges to leave the dressing room but he did ask for a few minutes silence, then he would lean against the wall and have some quiet moments to himself. If he could, he'd lock the door. He stayed with me for a few nights and he wanted to know if there was a Catholic Church in Clydach. We have a Church and a Convent and he was at Mass early on Sunday morning.

Hugh Banfield of the Welsh Referees' Society told me that his father was also two pounds and two ounces when he was born and he grew up to play second row for Loughor! We had a lot of support and help from family and friends. The consultant at the hospital informed me that we had come within an hour of losing Alison and forty minutes of losing Sam. I went cold at this and twenty-eight years of rugby experience paled into insignificance. I'm looking forward to being a fabulous grandfather!

The announcement about the award of the MBE was a real honour for me. I had received a letter from Downing Street some six weeks prior informing me that my name had been put forward by Hugh Banfield and Sir Tasker Watkins. The letter inquired that should the award be made, would I accept? Naturally my answer was in the affirmative. I didn't know whether or not it would happen, or when, and with everything that was happening with Alison and Samuel it was right at the back of my mind. I didn't mention it to anyone, not even to my Mother: you'd feel quite a fool if you told everyone and then nothing happened. It was, then, quite appropriate that Owen Jenkins, who has worked with me on this book, telephoned me with the news that I had been awarded an MBE. He was working in the BBC Newsroom in Cardiff and they had received an embargoed list of the Honours, the day before they would be made public. I genuinely didn't know! I was now free to tell Alison and my mother who immediately wanted to let everyone know. My mother was no stranger to news of this kind because my brother, Wyn, has also been awarded an MBE for his services to Trade Unionism – so a rare double for the Bevan family. It was in the papers the following day, a Saturday. That evening I attended a dinner at Penclawdd Rugby Club dinner and they presented me with a tankard with my name and the letters MBE engraved on it. When I went in to work the following Monday a new sign had been erected on my office door 'Derek Bevan MBE (Mediocre Baglan Electrician)'! It was certainly a period of highs and lows which distracted me from thinking about my retirement. It was when the list of referees for the Tri-Nations was issued and my name wasn't on it that it struck me quite hard that it was finally over.

2000-2001 – Retirement!

It was a strange feeling on the first Saturday of the 2000-01 season. I had recently moved house and since the weather was fine I painted the garden fence on the first day of the season. I didn't really have time to miss refereeing because there was so much to do around the house. For the first month I didn't see a game. This was retirement. Having said that, although I hadn't received a formal or structured approach from the WRU, I knew that the Welsh Referees' Society were keen to keep me involved in some way. But it was convenient for me not to be involved at the beginning of the season.

I had always said that I didn't think I would enjoy being an assessor of referees, there's too much administration in it. And it's not important to me how many scrums or lineouts there might have been in a game. I can watch a referee for twenty minutes and perhaps give some advice on the little things that could make him better. So if he's already a good referee I might help in some way to make him a great one. I certainly didn't intend putting myself forward to become a member of the WRU General Committee as I simply didn't have the time considering my work commitments. There was no conflict between Clive Norling and myself over this, though it did seem that there was something of a stand off between us. I wasn't asked and I didn't offer, so nobody made the first move. I suppose it was childish, really.

Hugh Banfield used his mediation skills and was instrumental in getting me involved again. Clive asked me to coach a group of hand picked, up-and-coming referees. There's no doubt that there are many coming forward and that the system for their progress is far better now. If referees produce the performances then they will certainly get on. Clive took me to matches for a month. This also persuaded Ken Parfitt, another ex-referee, to come back on board in a similar role. I had some misgivings. Modern refereeing can be like 'refereeing by numbers', everything by the book. I'd developed my own style over the years and I was slightly concerned that I was getting myself into something where I couldn't be myself. There are so many people qualified to assess these days that they're competing for places. Would they write reports which suit the IRB in order to maintain their position? The IRB has a Referee's Assessment Form – it's one of the most complicated forms I've ever seen. Every incident has to be counted. Referees can lose marks for not awarding a penalty at a collapsed scrum. This can encourage a referee to give a penalty even if they don't know who was responsible for the infringement. Some scrums go down accidentally, some go down for safety. I don't want to curtail individualism: if all referees are the same it will be like having a robot in the middle. It would be a pretty boring sport, too. You'll never have a game where a referee makes every decision correctly.

For our first game Clive, Ken and I watched a young referee at Dunvant. Clive took us through everything he wanted us to do – how to handle referees. I listened to him and took it all in, but I was already thinking about doing things my own way. What works for one 'coach' may not suit me. I always did things my own way when I refereed and I see no point in changing as a referees' coach. But I'm applying myself fully to the role and I get a tremendous amount of pleasure from seeing a referee improving. Equally, I will be annoyed with a young referee who isn't prepared to listen. Clive has targeted six to eight young referees with the aim of taking them as far as possible, hopefully to international level. They are all currently refereeing at First Division level so they're already well up the ladder. Now it's a case of helping to mould them into Premier referees and on from there. Our coaching form is a small one in comparison to the assessor's form. It takes only ten minutes after the game to complete, and highlights strong points, weaknesses and sets targets to be worked towards. Thankfully, no facts and figures are required about the game.

At one coaching session Clive told me that the IRB had

approached the WRU for suggestions for video referees. I had already heard from Nick Bunting of the RFU, who thought he was in a position to invite me to become a video ref. I was flattered to be asked by the Rugby Union but it led to some misunderstanding. It transpired that all video referees would be appointed by the IRB from names forwarded by the separate unions – just like on-field officials are. They were to be neutrals, like the on-field officials as it would be unfair to both the teams and the official himself to ask a local referee to rule on just the really crucial decisions.

The introduction of video referees is a further example of the professionalisation of the game and the resulting standard at which it is played now. Nick Mallett, the former coach of South Africa, thinks that the modern game is too quick for just one referee to control. So now we have five referees at international matches: the man in the middle, with the whistle; two touch judges who are also internationally qualified; the fourth official who controls substitutions, sin-bins and sendings-off; the video ref, who is an ex-international referee. The South Africa Rugby Union has been experimenting with two on-pitch referees. Tim Gresson, the New Zealander who is the IRB disciplinary chief has called for top matches to be controlled by two referees, one for set-pieces and one for general play. I don't know how this is going to work because you won't get two referees to agree in the bar after a game let alone in the middle of the park! It would have been interesting if Clive and I had had to share a game...

The WRU put forward two names to the IRB: Bob Yemen, one of our top assessors, and myself. We were both accepted, and the RFU invitation to be video ref for the game between England and World Champions Australia was withdrawn in line with the IRB rules. In the meantime I'd accepted an invitation to referee in the Golden Classics tournament in Bermuda – and this is retirement! Actually, the tournament has become increasingly serious and teams are going there to win now, rather than just enjoy themselves. South Africa, apart from a tough semifinal against the British Lions, won quite easily.

On my return a letter from the IRB informed me that I'd been appointed as video referee for the England-Argentina game at Twickenham on the 25th of November, which I naturally accepted.

Ironically, the match I'd been unofficially asked to video ref, England's victory over Australia, hinged on a video decision. Even with all the extra cameras installed for tryline incidents there's no guarantee that the video referee gets a better view than the on-field referee or touch judges. It's still the call of the man in the middle: he can take the advice of the video referee, or over-rule him as the video referee is there to offer an opinion. The video referee has strict guidelines and is called to comment on incidents to do with the goal line, touch in goal, dead ball and touch prior to the act of scoring a try or taking out the corner flag in the process of scoring. Incidents of foul play don't fall within his remit.

The use of video is another example of refereeing becoming easier. If there is any doubt over which way a decision should go the video ref can be called in. During the last game of the Tri-Nations between Australia and South Africa, Paul Honiss from New Zealand was referee and Nigel Whitehouse one of the touch judges. A close-run try was scored in the corner and 'Whitey' was on the spot to put up his thumb and pronounce 'Good try'. But the referee went to the video. Another Welsh touch judge was involved in the England vs Australia game. In the dying seconds Australia failed to find touch and England ran it back to score in the corner. Clayton nodded his head to signal the try but, yet again, the referee, Andre Watson this time, asked for confirmation from the video referee. This was Brian Stirling from Belfast. He'd had nothing to do all game, but now the match depended on his decision. The video reffing position at Twickenham is up on the same level as the hospitality boxes. The referee can watch the game through the glass window or on the television monitors in front of him. He can also hear everything the referee says to the players.

I wouldn't have liked to have been in Brian's shoes. There is no opt-out as video referee. But if you have a rolling maul crashing over the line and the cameras can't see for bodies whether the ball has been grounded then you have to be honest with the referee. I've seen the England-Australia incident three or four times and I'd go along with the call. I spoke with Brian the week following the game and he said that it was a strange feeling because, as he'd retired, he hadn't made a decision for nearly three years! He'd had a relaxing afternoon and was thinking of packing away his things at the end of the game. Quite possibly he'll never have to make another decision like that again. It gave victory to England by 22 points to 19.

England against Argentina was quite an easy afternoon for me and I wasn't called on to judge an incident. The match was played in atrocious conditions and, as a Welshman watching England play, it was boring! England won 19-0. But I certainly enjoyed the Friday night before the game with the match officials. Incidentally, video referees aren't paid, they receive travelling expenses and accommodation. I got another go as video referee in the Calcutta Cup game at Twickenham. Again I wasn't called upon but this time, I have to admit it, England were superb to watch, and won 43-3. I was also appointed for the Ireland against England fixture at the end of March, but the match was postponed because of the foot and mouth outbreak.

Being a video referee doesn't compare with being the referee in a game. I loved to be out in the middle. I didn't always like running touch and was often envious of the man with the whistle, though there were some games which were dire affairs and I was glad to be on the touch line. As a video referee there are butterflies in your stomach as a rolling maul approaches the try-line, but for ninety per cent of the game you're relaxed and enjoying it.

When the referee appointments for the Six Nations were announced I was amazed that there were no Welsh referees on the list, particularly as Italy's presence meant more games. I believe that ageism has crept in. There are good referees who might be doing very well but now don't seem to progress because of their age. There were no Six Nations fixtures for Clayton Thomas, Ed Morrison, Jim Fleming, Colin Hawke and Wayne Ericsson. But I was pleased when Robert Davies was called in to referee the Calcutta Cup when Paddy O'Brien had to withdraw through injury. Robert did a marvellous job and fully deserved the plaudits he was given.

The original decision not to include a Welsh referee was, for me, a political one. Welsh referees had performed well in the European cup competitions, but the IRB was sending out a message to Wales that it lacked a professional refereeing structure. Similarly Scotland and Italy, who also didn't have any referees in the Six Nations. The WRU has since taken steps to introduce professional referees. I still have reservations about professionalism.

Wales is still addressing some of the issues bound up in professional refereeing. What happens as a professional referee if you lose some form or break a leg? There must be a good contract and guaranteed income. Some young referees will have to consider switching from their present career to one as a referee. Can they go back if it doesn't work out? In the course of a match referees will have to be careful to concentrate on the game itself rather than trying to get a top mark from the assessor to secure their future. The stamp of a good referee is whether or not he has the respect of the players. If two sides are ready to play rugby, the game benefits from a liberal interpretation of the laws. An assessor with the law book in his hands can probably knock holes in the referee's performance but if the players come off saying they've really enjoyed the game, then isn't that something as well? In some matches I ignored minor infringements to allow the game to flow. Equally I came down hard on teams who didn't want to play rugby. The referee must be able to adjust to his part in the game. The real difficulty arises when one side wants to play and the other just wants to spoil. This can lead to frustration and foul play which gives the referee major problems. I don't believe current referees should be used as assessors to judge the performance of their peers.

Away from the game I had an MBE to collect. I had planned to take my mother and my daughter Alison with me to London. Mum had bought a new outfit especially for the event and was looking forward immensely to her day at the Palace. But she came down with a dreadful chest ailment and was advised by her doctor not to travel. It took some gloss off the occasion but my sister, Anne, came in as first reserve.

I was to receive the MBE on Tuesday 10 October so the three of us travelled up the day before and stayed in an hotel so we could enjoy ourselves. The day itself was cold and miserable as we took a taxi to Buckingham Palace. We had our tickets and instructions where to go, who to speak to and what to do when we arrived. I'd hired a morning suit but I didn't know what would happen during the ceremony itself. We showed our passes at the gate and joined the queue of people waiting to go inside. I recognised some from the sporting and business world; David Rowe-Beddoe, the Chairman of the Welsh Development Agency, was there to receive a knighthood.

We were ushered into the main hall and split up, recipients to one side, the guests to the other. There was another series of checks before we proceeded into a gallery adorned by magnificent portraits of former kings and queens. There were roped-off sections for the different categories of awards, and refreshments and the opportunity to mingle and chat. Then a Palace official told us what to do in the ceremony. He assured us it would go like clockwork and we would be taken in ten at a time. We were shown how to walk forward when our names were called, turn left, bow and walk up to the Queen. She would place the award on a special pin and have a quick chat before shaking our hand, the signal to step backwards, bow and leave. There would be officials present in the room to help if you forgot the protocol.

There were television monitors in the waiting room on which we watched the knighthoods. I started to think about what I would say to the Queen, or should I let her say something first? She might want to chat about something totally different! I had met Princess Anne on four occasions, and Prince Charles and Prince Edward, so there was plenty I could talk about, and that was just her family. She might want to know about mine!

Things were getting closer as they went through the OBEs. Then there were bravery awards. When I saw a soldier in a wheelchair, with no legs I felt humble – I was getting an award for blowing a whistle. Now it was our turn, and as a Bevan I was in the first group of ten. As instructed, we followed the Palace official and stopped out of sight of the Queen until our names were called. One by one we moved forward until the official had his hand across my chest. He turned to me and said, "I know you, you're a referee. It's about time you got some recognition. We've got one of your lads from Welsh rugby in the next session." That was Neil Jenkins. I heard "William Derek Bevan", the official removed his hand and I was off. The announcer continued, "For services to Welsh Rugby". My stomach was really turning. I was much more nervous than I had been before any international. As I walked along the red carpet I saw Alison and Anne before I saw the Queen. They had great seats towards the front of the first guests' section.

The Queen had an aide next to her who was whispering in her ear as I approached. Either side was a Ghurka. Security was very low key: there were guards with swords upright to their noses who could leap into action. I remembered all my instructions, walked forward and bowed. The Queen leaned forward and placed the MBE on the clip and asked if I'd come up that morning. I replied that we had travelled the day before. She then said, "You're a rugby referee – that's the game my grandson plays." I replied, "I've had the pleasure of refereeing your grandson in Bridgend." Then she asked me at what level I refereed – so she obviously didn't remember the World Cup Final! I said I'd been an international referee. She smiled and said, "You've been called a few names then!" Then she shook my hand which, of course, was the signal for me to leave. We'd been told not to linger. She'd already been on her feet for an hour and a half and there were still plenty of awards to go. It was a firm handshake and off I went. I took five paces backwards, bowed, turned to the right and walked out. I was greeted by another official who threw the clip into a box, took the award and placed it in a presentation box. I was given all the paperwork about the ceremony and awards, and details of how to purchase a video or photographs of the event. There was also a list of all the recipients that day. After that I was able to join the audience for the remainder of the ceremony. The band had been playing quietly in the background throughout proceedings and when all the awards had been given it struck up 'God Save the Queen', which we all sang. I joined up with Alison and Anne and we went outside to take our own photos. It was bitterly cold, so we didn't take long before hopping into a taxi to the hotel and changing for the journey home. "Mam would have loved this!" said Anne. I checked my pocket every now and then to make sure the award was still there!

I was still busy on the field. The following month I travelled to Singapore for an international sevens tournament, where I teamed up with Paddy O'Brien. It was a great competition, organised by the Singapore Cricket Club at the Padang ground. There were teams from Asia, Army teams from the UK and clubs from Australia and New Zealand. Randwick were there from Sydney, with coach David Campese. I knew what to expect – high temperatures and humidity, and when there are clubs from Australia and New Zealand involved you have to be ready for anything. I refereed the Plate Final between Hong Kong and Petone from New Zealand, who won.

Back at home Christmas 2000 was a very special one for the family. My grandson Samuel had progressed very well. At one stage we didn't think he would, but we had a great Christmas with him. I gave him some rugby kit and a pair of shorts from Bermuda! I'm really enjoying being a grandfather.

Rugby has been a great game for me. I've no regrets about the decisions I've made and have made them in places I never imagined I would visit. I would have loved to have refereed the British Lions – as I'm sure every British referee would – but neutrality ruled it out. I don't thing I've missed out on anything: I've done all the major rugby nations and most of the merging ones. And unusually, I've had the pleasure of refereeing Wales twice. A New Zealand or Australian referee doesn't get the opportunity of refereeing a Bledisloe Cup match so I've been lucky to do that and referee my own country.

I haven't decided whether being a video referee is for me yet but I still enjoy doing the LloydsTSB Schoolboy League when I'm asked. I can only thank my fellow Welsh Panel referees, who I've had the pleasure of working with over my career: Clayton Thomas, Clive Norling, Gareth Simmonds, Bob Yemen, Les Peard, Robert Davies, Ken Rowlands, David Davies, Nigel Whitehouse and most importantly of all Winston Jones, probably the greatest loss to Welsh referees. Winston was a man who never let you down, and was a man who didn't know how to say no. His funeral still remains the blackest day I have experienced in Welsh Rugby. I would particularly like to express my gratitude to Vardre Rugby Club and Evan Dan Williams who started it all for me

I've made a lot of friends and even some enemies along the way. But for each person that I didn't get on with there must be twenty-five friends all over the world who've been gained through rugby – not a bad score. When I look back over what must be around two thousand games I could take out just two dozen that, with hindsight, I wouldn't have wanted to have been involved in. One player accused me of costing his team's win bonus! I'd do it all again if I could, starting right at the very bottom. At the 2000 Cwmtawe

Sevens I was quite jealous of the young guys now coming through and what they have in front of them. I would encourage anyone to go for it. It's been great.

Postscript: Jim Fleming

I suppose that the refereeing careers of Derek and myself run somewhat in parallel. We were both appointed to our respective International Panels at the same time and both refereed our first major internationals in 1985. Since then we have appeared at all four Rugby World Cups, the only two referees to have achieved such a feat.

It's amazing to think that in the fifteen or sixteen years since our paths first touched that we have only officiated together twice. First, we were the touch judges in the 1987 World Cup semifinal between Australia and France in Sydney, while some years later, Derek ran touch for me when Argentina played the Barbarians at Cardiff.

There are many stories that I could relate about Derek, some of which already appear within this book, others which cannot be mentioned for whatever reason, but one which is of particular significance to me directly happened during the 1999 Rugby World Cup in Wales. Derek and I were there and were probably looked upon as two referees of the old school. Two of the very small number of referees at RWC who were not full time and who still enjoyed the odd pint in the evening. I had gone to Cardiff happy to be selected and hoping, at the outside, to get a quarter final match. Derek, I know, felt the same way about his own involvement.

Well as things progressed it appeared that both he and I were refereeing pretty well and both of us got quarter final games. After my game between South Africa and England I felt that I had a reasonable chance of making the final. A few assessors expressed the same view.

On the day the appointment of the semifinal referees was made, Derek was given the Australia vs South Africa game and I was handed the New Zealand vs France game, not bad for two 'old timers'. Derek was delighted, as was I, but I was somewhat sad to realise that my chance of the final had gone.

Derek was obviously aware of what was going through my mind. He came over to me and I still remember his words. "I never thought," he said to me, "that one referee would be over the moon at being appointed to a semifinal, and the other would be gutted. Let's go for a couple of pints." Well the couple of pints turned into more than a few and we visited some of Cardiff's best. I remember the Ship and Pilot as well as some gay bar somewhere. Derek spent the next few hours lifting my spirits, in more ways than one, without giving a thought to his own marvellous appointment.

Derek's actions summed him up in my eyes. Although he had been appointed to another great game of rugby, his first thoughts were not for himself, but for someone else. It's the same on the rugby field. He's not on the field for himself, but to help others enjoy themselves, although he obviously enjoys what he does and what he has achieved.

He's one of life's gentlemen, someone who has a feel for life as well as a feel for rugby. I count it an honour to be numbered as one of his friends, a friendship that I am sure will continue for many years to come.

Postscript: Steve Bale

Those of us with as long a memory as Derek Bevan's can remember him in the long-lost days before he was an international referee, though thank goodness there are fewer of us who remember him as a Vardre flanker.

It is now very nearly sixteen years since a thirty-six-year-old referee caught the eye by sending off a twenty-year-old Pontypool lock by the name of Kevin Moseley, and if big Kevin had the last laugh it is only because he was still playing (for Penzance & Newlyn) when Derek finally buried his whistle. The point is that that dismissal said everything anyone would ever need to know about Bevan, and I am happy to relate that not only your *Western Mail* reporter but also our photographer was present at Newbridge Welfare Ground to record the defining moment. The picture – featured on the jacket of this book – is a beauty, Bevan pointing with his right arm at the disconsolate and incredulous Moseley and with his left towards the dressing-rooms. It was 30 December 1983 and even without Moseley, Pooler went on to win a highly charged affair by 34-13. His offence was to swing a foot at one Andy Stimpson. He had to go. He did.

I don't know if Derek still has that photograph among his collection but he was mildly embarrassed when that self-same *Western Mail* reporter suggested he might care for a copy – as if to say, why would anyone want to bother with him? This, as Louis Luyt might have bothered to find out, was a man who never wanted any gift other than that of contributing to the game. Equally, Bevan was never reluctant to send someone off if it was deserved, always regretful that it had had to happen. That is what that picture, and his response to it, will for ever mean to me. As for Luyt, he was actually right about Derek Bevan, but for entirely the wrong reasons, when he described our man as "the most wonderful ref in the world". Trouble was the South African RFU President based his judgement on Bevan's handling of the 1995 World Cup semifinal in which the Springboks beat France. If he had been talking about his entire career, no one would have argued.

Luyt gave Bevan a watch, and the joke took four years for its punchline when the 1999 semifinal between South Africa and Australia ran to 10 minutes' stoppage-time after three had been announced. Derek, where is the Louis Luyt watch? we all asked. Bevan could have been excused for being offended, both by Luyt and by everyone else's reaction to Luyt's reaction to him. But that has always been the thing about Derek, and the reason he became and remained a genuinely "wonderful ref". He never took himself too seriously, always admitted his mistakes and never, ever exaggerated his own role in a game. Even his personal Everest, the 1991 World Cup final between England and Australia, proved as much. "There are going to be some of the world's most talented players on view at Twickenham and after it's all over I will just be happy if everyone is talking about them and the game rather than me," he told me on the eve of the final.

Right enough. When he whistled his very first match, Cwmgors vs Trebanos 2nd XVs no less, a spectator advised him: "Bevan, you were bloody useless as a player, and you're bloody useless as a referee." He tells this story against himself, but the rest of the world came to disagree.

INDEX

Matches referred to in the text